## *Crossway Bible Guide*

Series editors: Ian Coffey (NT), Stephen Gaukroger (OT)
Old Testament editor: Stephen Dray
New Testament editor: Steve Motyer

## Titles in this series

*Genesis*, Richard and Tricia Johnson
*Exodus*, Stephen Dray
*Leviticus*, Derek Tidball
*Joshua*, Charles Price
*Ruth and Esther*, Debra Reid
*Ezra and Nehemiah*, Dave Cave
*Psalms 1 – 72*, Alan Palmer
*Psalms 73 – 150*, Alan Palmer and Debra Reid
*Isaiah*, Philip Hacking
*Daniel*, Stephen Gaukroger
*Six Minor Prophets*, Michael Wilcock
*Haggai, Zechariah and Malachi*, John James
*Matthew's Gospel*, Stephen Dray
*Mark's Gospel*, David Hewitt
*Luke's Gospel*, Simon Jones
*John's Gospel*, Ian Barclay
*Acts*, Stephen Gaukroger
*Romans*, David Coffey
*1 Corinthians*, Stephen Dray and Robin Dowling
*2 Corinthians*, Jonathan Lamb
*Galatians*, Simon Jones
*Ephesians*, Steve Motyer
*Philippians*, Ian Coffey
*Colossians and Philemon*, Stephen Gaukroger and
  Derek Wood
*1 & 2 Thessalonians*, Alec Motyer and Steve Motyer
*Timothy and Titus*, Michael Griffiths
*Hebrews*, Steve Motyer
*James*, David Field
*Peter and Jude*, Dianne Tidball
*1, 2, 3 John*, Dianne Tidball
*Revelation*, Peter Hicks

*The Bible with Pleasure*, Steve Motyer
*Discovering the Old Testament*, Alec Motyer
*Discovering the New Testament*, Simon Jones
*Housegroups: The Leaders' Survival Guide*, Ian Coffey and
  Stephen Gaukroger (eds.)

*Peter and Jude:*
*Crossway Bible Guide*

**Dianne Tidball**

Crossway Books Nottingham

CROSSWAY BOOKS
*Norton Street, Nottingham NG7 3HR, England*
*Email: ivp@ivpbooks.com*
*Website: www.ivpbooks.com*

*First published 2007*

**British Library Cataloguing in Publication Data**
A catalogue record for this book is available from the British Library.

ISBN 978–1–85684–228–0

Set in Palatino
Typeset in Great Britain by Avocet Typeset, Chilton, Aylesbury, Bucks
Printed and bound in Great Britain by Creative Print and Design (Wales), Ebbw Vale

Dedicated to Beryl Gray,
encourager, supporter and Mum

# CONTENTS

# Welcome!

These days, meeting together to study the Bible in groups appears to be a booming leisure-time activity in many parts of the world. In the United Kingdom alone, it is estimated that over one million people each week meet in home Bible-study groups.

This series has been designed to help such groups and, in particular, those who lead them. These Bible Guides are also very suitable for individual study, and may help hard-pressed preachers, teachers and students too (see 'How to use this Bible Guide', p. 10).

We have therefore enlisted authors who are in the business of teaching the Bible to others and are doing it well. They have kept in their sights two clear aims:

1. To explain and apply the message of the Bible in non-technical language.

2. To encourage discussion, prayer and action on what the Bible teaches.

All of us engaged in the project believe that the Bible is the Word of God – given to us in order that people might discover him and his purposes for our lives. We believe that the sixty-six books which go to make up the Bible, although written by different people, in different places, at different times, through different circumstances, have a single unifying theme: that theme is Salvation. This means free forgiveness and the removal of all our guilt, it means the gift of eternal life, and it means the wholeness of purpose and joy which God has designed us to experience here and now, all of this being made possible through the Lord Jesus Christ.

# How to use this Bible Guide

These guides have been prepared both for personal study and for the leaders and members of small groups. More information about group study follows on the next few pages.

You can use this book very profitably as a personal study guide. The short studies are ideal for daily reading: the first of the questions provided is usually aimed to help you with personal reflection (see 'How to tackle personal Bible study'). If you prefer to settle down to a longer period of study, you can use groups of three to five studies, and thus get a better overview of a longer Bible passage. In either case, using the Bible Guide will help you to be disciplined about regular study, a habit that countless Christians have found greatly beneficial.

Yet a third use for these Bible Guides is as a quarry for ideas for the busy Bible teacher, providing outlines and application for those giving talks or sermons or teaching children. You will need more than this book can offer, of course, but the way the Bible text is broken down, comments are offered and questions are raised may well suggest directions to follow.

## How to tackle personal Bible study

We have already suggested that you might use this book as a personal study guide. Now for some more detail.

One of the best methods of Bible study is to read the text through carefully several times, possibly using different versions or translations. Having reflected on the material, it is a good discipline to write down your own thoughts before doing anything else. At this stage it can be useful to consult another background book. See 'For further reading' on page 144. If you are using this book as your main study resource, then read through the relevant sections carefully, turning up the Bible references that are mentioned. The questions at the end of each chapter are specifically designed to help you to apply the passage to your own situation. You may find it helpful to write your answers to the questions in your notes.

It is a good habit to conclude with prayer, bringing before God the things you have learned.

If this kind of in-depth study is too demanding for you and you have only a short time at your disposal, read the Bible passage, read the comments in the Bible Guide, think round one of the questions and commit what you have learned to God in a brief prayer. This would take about fifteen minutes without rushing it.

### How to tackle your group Bible study

#### 1. Getting help

If you are new to leading groups, you will obviously want to get all the help you can from ministers and experienced friends. Books are also extremely helpful and we strongly recommend a book prepared by the editors of this series of Bible Guides: *Housegroups: The Leaders' Survival Guide*, edited by Ian Coffey and Stephen Gaukroger (Crossway Books, 1996). This book looks at the whole range of different types of group, asking what is the point of it all, what makes a good leader, how to tackle your meeting, how to help the members, how to study, pray, share and worship, and plenty of other pointers, tips and guidelines.

This book is a 'must' for all leaders of small groups. It is written by a team of people widely experienced in this area. It is available at your local Christian bookshop. If you have difficulty in obtaining a copy, write to Crossway Books, Norton Street, Nottingham NG7 3HR, UK.

## 2. Planning a programme with your Bible Guide

This guide is a commentary on God's Word, written to help group members to get the most out of their studies. Although it is never ideal to chop up Scripture into small pieces, which its authors never intended, huge chunks are indigestible and so we have tried to provide a diet of bite-sized mouthfuls.

If you want to get an overview of the Bible book in a series of meetings, you will need to select appropriate studies for each meeting. Read them yourself first and prepare a short summary of the studies you are tackling for your group. Ideally you could write it on a sheet of A5 paper and hand a copy to each member.

If you do not intend to cover the whole Bible book, choose a series of studies to suit the number of meetings you have available. It is a good idea to use consecutive studies, not to dodge about. You will then build up a detailed picture of one section of Scripture.

## 3. Preparing to lead

Reading, discussing with friends, studying, praying, reflecting on life ... preparation can be endless. But do not be daunted by that. If you wait to become the perfect leader you will never start at all. The really vital elements in preparation are:

▶ prayer (not only in words but an attitude of dependence on God: 'Lord, I can't manage this on my own')

▶ familiarity with the study passage (careful reading of the text, the Bible Guide study and any other resource books that throw light on it) and

▶ a clear idea of where you hope to get in the meeting (notes on your introduction, perhaps, recap what was covered at the last meeting, and what direction you hope the questions will take you in – don't force the group to give your answers).

Here is a short checklist for the busy group leader:

Have I prayed about the meeting?

What do I want to achieve through the meeting?

Have I prepared the material?

Am I clear about the questions that will encourage positive group discussion?

Am I gently encouraging silent members?

Am I, again gently, quietening the chatterers?

Am I willing to admit ignorance?

Am I willing to listen to what the group members say and to value their contributions?

Am I ready not to be dogmatic, not imposing my ideas on the group?

Have I planned how to involve the members in discovering for themselves?

Have I developed several 'prayer points' that will help focus the group?

Are we applying Scripture to our experience of real life or only using it as a peg to hang our opinions on?

Are we finding resources for action and change or just having a nice talk?

Are we all enjoying the experience together?

# Finding your way around this book

**In our Bible Guides we have developed special symbols to make things easier to follow. Every study therefore has an opening section which is the passage in a nutshell.**

The main section is the one that makes sense of the passage.

## Questions

Every passage also has special questions for personal and group study after the main section. Some questions are addressed to us as individuals, some speak to us as members of our church or home group, while others concern us as members of God's people worldwide. The questions are deliberately designed

▶ to get people thinking about the passage

▶ to apply the text to 'real-life' situations

▶ to encourage reflection, discussion and action!

As a group leader you may well discover additional questions that will have special relevance to your group, so look out for these and note them in your preparation time.

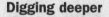

### Digging deeper

Some passages require an extra amount of explanation, and we have put these sections into different categories. The first kind gives additional background material that helps us to understand something factual. For example, if we dig deeper into the Gospels, it helps us to know who the Pharisees were, so that we can see more easily why they related to Jesus in the way they did. These technical sections are marked with a spade.

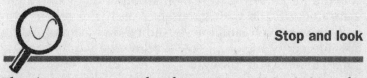

### Stop and think

This feature appears with passages which highlight important themes or teaching. Bible references and questions will help you think them through.

### Stop and look

This feature gives us the chance to stand back from the action and take stock. It gives a summary of what to look for in the passages we are about to read, and useful background material.

# Comments from the author
# for readers today

As you use this guide, I hope you will share a little of the pleasure I have gained from studying and reflecting on the letters of Peter and Jude. This guide seeks to bring alive the context in which the letters were written and the context in which they were received, so that we can understand as fully as possible the meaning for us today. I am grateful to so many commentators and friends over a number of years, who have shaped my thinking, and I hope the words I have used might help in some small way to shape others in godly character and life. However, I apologize if having benefited from the thoughts of others I have unwittingly been over-reliant on them.

As you study and reflect on the words of Scripture and my words as the author of this Bible Guide, try hard to let the Holy Spirit mould your thinking and reflection, so that these might not just be words, but food for the soul. Peter and Jude both wrote to real situations, where Christians were doing battle with themselves and with others. You will find yourself similarly wrestling and at times being bewildered by life at all levels; allow the words of these letters to help you through.

Parts of these letters are clearly straightforward and easy to apply in theory, and yet hard to maintain in practice. Our weak and feeble character lets us down far too often. Other parts of these letters are much harder to understand and therefore to apply, such as Peter speaking of Jesus preaching to the dead, and the comments of Peter and Jude to do with judgment and punishment. Don't give up too easily; there is some truth in the saying 'There is no gain without pain.' Be prepared to think deeply and grapple with God as Jacob did (Genesis 32:22–30), so that you are stronger and better equipped as a disciple of Christ.

# Routes through the letters of Peter and Jude

## 1. Learning about God – Father, Son and Holy Spirit

Living hope in tough times: 1 Peter 1:1–5
Be sure: evidence from the apostles and prophets:
    2 Peter 1:12–21
Money, sex, power and judgment: 2 Peter 2:1–10a
A salutary reminder: 2 Peter 3:1–10
A golden hello! Jude 1–2
A golden goodbye! Jude 24–25

## 2. Suffering

Salvation: past, present and future: 1 Peter 1:6–12
The power of Christ's suffering: 1 Peter 3:17–22
Chosen for the narrow path: 1 Peter 4:12–19

## 3. Discipleship training

Holy living: 1 Peter 1:13–21
The best diet for the born again: 1 Peter 1:22 – 2:3
Spiritual stones: 1 Peter 2:4–10
Final advice and farewell: 1 Peter 5:8–14
Make every effort: 2 Peter 1:1–11
Live well now and live for ever: 2 Peter 3:11–18
How we can thrive: Jude 17–23

## 4. Community life

Living within godless structures: 1 Peter 2:11–17
Godly common sense and good living: 1 Peter 3:8–16
Living in a pleasure obsessed world: 1 Peter 4:1–11
Leadership in the church: 1 Peter 5:1–7
Warning: false teaching could damage your health:
    Jude 8–16

# CHRISTIANS UNDER THREAT

## 1 Peter

# 1 Peter 1:1–5

Living hope in tough times

---

**Peter begins his letter with a blessing and a reminder of the blessings of belonging to Christ. He then speaks of the hope that every believer has, even in times of trial.**

---

Can you imagine being in a situation of persecution and struggle; without email or telephone and little contact and encouragement from others; wondering whether what you believe is true; wrestling with whether it is all worth it; and thinking you never thought it would be this difficult? And then, imagine receiving a letter that encourages you and reminds you that you are not forgotten, that what you believe and hope is shared by many others and is based on eyewitness evidence, clear prophetic words and the person of Jesus Christ himself. That is how it was for the original readers of this letter. It could be that as you read these words you are finding spiritual life difficult and you can identify with the first readers of Peter's letters. Maybe if you are not struggling, then you can still recognize that many Christians do face daily harassment because of their faith, and need the reassurance of this letter.

Peter begins with a traditional format that would be common at the time. First, he makes it clear who is sending the letter: much more sensible than our custom of putting the name at the end, so you may have to read a couple of pages before you know who is writing to you. Secondly, he identifies the recipients of the letter, and finally, he greets them in terms that hold depths of meaning and Christian truth.

The second part of the greeting introduces many of the

themes he will write about in greater detail later. These conventions are followed by the apostle Paul in his letters. It is as if the first verses after the greeting are a preview or taster of what is to come.

Having identified himself as an apostle, one who is set apart to found the church, Peter greets his readers as 'elect' and 'strangers', establishing both their spiritual heritage and their social isolation. All who have responded to Christ have been chosen by God, elected by him, and while it might seem that the individual makes a personal decision to respond, it is God who has selected them. This is an encouragement and a comfort. It is always discouraging to be left out, whether it is the cricket team or the choir, and it is always an encouragement to be chosen, and when that choice is made by God himself, it brings added comfort and gratification. He identifies his readers as those who live in scattered communities of the region today known as Turkey.

Peter refers to the Christian readers as 'strangers in the world'. Such a phrase would have been understood in terms of their low social status and their Christian faith. It seems likely that Peter had in mind that he was writing not only to slaves and wives (which he mentions later in the letter) and others with little social influence or protection under the law, but also to those who had the added social isolation of faith, which would have been viewed with suspicion by most in society. It is reasonable to assume that Peter writes not to wealthy and powerful Christians, but to poor and marginalized believers, encouraging them that they are chosen by God and made holy by the work of the Holy Spirit in their lives through the death of Christ, to whom they have responded in obedience and faith.

As a warm and generous pastor, Peter shares a blessing with his readers. He wants them to know all the kindness and goodness of God and the fullness of reconciliation with him, with all the personal and social significance that has. He doesn't just seek this in a measured way but in abundance (verse 2).

Peter moves from the opening words to a positive and inspirational thought about hope and salvation (verses 3–6), before addressing other issues. Peter is definitely a 'cup half full' not a 'cup half empty' sort of person. He is aware of troubles, but he is much more conscious of God's purposes and plans and all that has been achieved through Jesus Christ. The excitement and pulsing energy of these words is almost tangible. Peter exuberantly gives thanks for the new life and hope that Christians have because of the death and resurrection of Christ. He lays clear foundations on which other teaching will be built. He speaks of the mercy of God, a reminder that God is gracious and kind, and does not deal with people as they deserve. He mentions a living hope – the expectation that God is fulfilling his purposes and they will be achieved, which gives realistic optimism despite the present circumstances.

Peter links all these together as a chain reaction: God's generous mercy leads to spiritual rebirth, which brings hope in the present of a future inheritance. This inheritance that God's people who have faith in Jesus Christ can expect is life with God beyond death: a fully realized relationship with God; all the riches of a new heaven and a new earth; the spiritual treasure of which Jesus also speaks (Luke 12:32–34). Unlike inheritances in this life, these can never fade, corrode or rot. Those who have found faith have tasted of this spiritual inheritance; they have had an advance but the full realization of this inheritance is yet to come.

However, no inheritance is of any value if the beneficiary does not live to enjoy it. Peter seems to understand the struggle that faith and belief can be at times. It would be an unusual Christian who didn't at some time wrestle with issues, and wonder whether they would end faithfully and obediently as servants of Christ. Peter reminds them that their faith does not depend on them holding on to belief against all the opposition and struggles, but on God shielding and protecting them until his plans are fulfilled.

## Questions

1. Does the fact that God has chosen you give you encouragement and a sense of worth?
2. Is the church today too at-home in the world and not as distinctive as strangers should be?
3. How can God's foreknowledge be understood alongside free will?

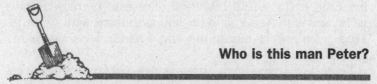

**Who is this man Peter?**

Peter, the named author of this letter, was called by Jesus to be one of the original disciples. He was named Simon, but early on Jesus gave him the new name Peter (Greek) or Cephas (Aramaic) (John 1:42). His brother was Andrew, his father is named as Jonah (Matthew 16:17), and his family's hometown was Bethsaida near the north shore of the Sea of Tiberias. His brother Andrew was a disciple of John the Baptist (John 1:40), and it is therefore likely that Peter came under the influence of John the Baptist's teaching.

Peter was a fisherman, who had no formal education and astonished his listeners when he could speak and preach with understanding and knowledge. According to Mark 1:30 and 1 Corinthians 9:5, he was married, but we don't know if he had children.

Peter was one of the three who made up the inner circle of Jesus' disciples. In the Garden of Gethsemane (Matthew 26:37) and at the Mount of Transfiguration (Matthew 17:1), Peter, James and John were present when other disciples were not, and Peter acts as the spokesperson on behalf of the other disciples on a number of occasions (e.g. Matthew 18:21). He had a key role in the forty days between the resurrection and ascension of Christ, giving a lead and being a witness to the empty tomb, which means he is often recognized as the leader amongst the disciples.

The character and personality of Peter have been scrutinized more than most. He is traditionally known as impetuous, spontaneous and a man of action. This comes from incidents such as the occasion when he cut off the ear of the high priest's servant (John 18:10–11), and when he committed to laying down his life for Jesus (John 13:37) and then denied him three times shortly afterwards.

Character matures and changes over the years, and by the time Peter wrote his letters, he was more senior in years and experience, and his letters indicate a more measured response to situations and greater wisdom in his actions.

Peter led the church, having been commissioned by Jesus for a particular role in establishing the church. This is one area of significant difference between Protestant and Roman Catholic doctrine. While evangelicals consider Peter's role as significant in founding the church, there is no clear biblical evidence for assuming a succession from Peter for those in leadership. Roman Catholics have based their doctrine of the Pope and apostolic succession on the belief that Peter and those who followed him are commissioned to have specific authority in the church in every generation.

After the ascension of Jesus, Peter takes a major lead in the founding of the church (Acts 1:15), and he is the primary preacher (Acts 2:14), as well as speaking before the Jewish authorities (Acts 4:8) and presiding over issues of spiritual discipline (Acts 5:3). Miraculous powers are attributed to him (Acts 5:15) and he is the first to take the gospel intentionally to Gentiles (Acts 10:1–48). The issue of Gentiles within the church caused controversy, as the church adjusted to understanding the purposes of God through Christ to include people of all nations and races.

It is difficult to keep track of Peter's travels as he preached and shared the gospel. He has been traced to Caesarea, but he was also imprisoned in Jerusalem (Acts 12:17). After he escaped imprisonment he went elsewhere, but the place has not been identified. At some point Peter went to Antioch (Galatians 2:11), and possibly to Corinth, and he may have been working in Bithynia (Acts 16:7).

At the time of writing his first letter, Peter was in Rome and under arrest. Shortly after writing what we know as his second letter, he was killed at the hands of the Roman Emperor Nero, whose reputation for persecution and execution of Christians is well documented. This fulfilled the words of Jesus in John 21:18, that in his old age he would be taken where he did not want to go and be led by others.

## 1:6–12

### Salvation: past present and future

**Peter recognizes the tension of living in the present with a hope of full salvation still to come. The trials of the present are not comfortable but they are worth it.**

For some people a good weekend is spoilt by thinking about work on Monday morning. For others, the great beauty of the rainforests is marred by the pollution that is damaging them. For many, occasions of great hope and inspiration are ruined by worries or problems. In a similar but greater way, Peter realizes that there is a huge contrast between the great salvation that believers have in Christ, and their present circumstances. They rejoice in the wonder of God and his power and all he has achieved through the death and resurrection of Christ, but still they face the daily grind of struggling to survive, of being opposed by those around, and of being oppressed by the ungodly culture of which they are a part.

The struggles faced by the church communities in Turkey at this time were not outright persecution, such as occurred later in the century under the Emperors Nero and Domitian, but Christians were harassed and misunderstood, which created difficulties and pressure.

Difficult times can be good for us, but it never feels as if they are. I recall facing a particularly harsh set of circumstances, feeling hurt, misled, unfairly treated and discouraged. I went to good friends to receive solace and comfort, and their response was 'It's all character building.' They were right, but at that moment I didn't want my character built.

If we are to grow in faith, challenging situations are necessary to refine and to show up weak areas. If all that Christians ever required was handed to them on a plate, there would be no need to trust God or to develop faith in him. Wrestling and being tested are necessary, just as gold is refined with heat and fire to increase its purity and remove contamination. Faith is refined by various circumstances to remove ideas, thoughts and qualities of character that pollute and contaminate the life of God in us. As Peter notes, faith is much more important than gold and so being refined, although not easy, should be recognized as valuable and positive.

As Peter continues in his thoughts and encouragement to the scattered believers, he captures the tension of faith now and faith not yet. When Christ returns and their faith is shown to be genuine, there will be praise and delight all round, but that is in the future. In the present, alongside the hardship and testing, the relationship of love already exists. Even though Jesus has not yet returned and they have not seen him, still they have faith, they believe in his presence, they trust in his teaching and are filled with delight and pleasure in their relationship with him. Of course, the readers of this letter would not have seen Jesus in person, unlike Peter who lived with him and knew him closely for three years. While the completion of their salvation remains in the future, they are daily receiving the blessings of salvation from God through his Spirit.

Every day they are forgiven and provided for, and receive God's grace for all their needs.

The opening verses of this letter, following the greeting, begin as a prayer of praise and thanksgiving, but as the thoughts are developed, so the verses take on much more the character of teaching and instruction. Having mentioned their eternal inheritance and acknowledged the trials that they currently face, Peter continues with the theme of salvation, reminding his readers that while the completion of that salvation is in the future, the fruits of salvation are a present reality.

Peter keeps to the theme of salvation in verses 10–12, and his comments are insightful for understanding how the early Christians viewed the Old Testament and how they handled it. The Old Testament prophets such as Isaiah and Jeremiah spoke of the salvation that would come through Christ (e.g. Isaiah 9; Jeremiah 31) and of the relationship of the nation of Israel to God. They tried to understand God's purposes and plans, to comprehend timescales, and it was the same Holy Spirit who had worked in Christ, who was guiding their thinking and searching. They knew their words had a purpose way beyond themselves; they were foretelling the gospel that would be preached by the apostles and other evangelists once Jesus the Messiah had accomplished his work of death and resurrection.

The Old Testament is highly regarded by New Testament writers and by Jesus himself. It is frequently quoted and its teaching is reinforced by early church leaders. Occasionally I come across church communities who place little emphasis on the Old Testament. They assume that the important teaching and comment is in the New Testament. To neglect the Old Testament is to miss out on a rich source of encouragement, inspiration and deep understanding of God's character and qualities and his purposes through history. Peter certainly reinforced the importance of understanding the Old Testament, and that is a good example for the church today.

## Questions

1. Reflect on what salvation means for you in the present and in the future.
2. Does the church give adequate emphasis to the Old Testament – what does it gain if it does?
3. Does suffering always bring about the positive effect of refining faith?

# 1 Peter 1:13–21

## Holy living

**Peter gives clear advice on how to be holy, and this holiness he encourages is rich and rewarding in every way.**

I often think that holiness gets a bad press; it sounds so boring, and yet the holiest people I have known have been full of laughter, humour, fun and joy.
There has been a generosity of character about them and a warmth of personality that is winsome and appealing. I think the generally negative view of holiness is because some of us grew up with the idea that being a faithful disciple of Jesus is about 'not sinning', and that usually involved exhortations from senior members of the church community not to drink alcohol, smoke tobacco or watch inappropriate TV. (Drugs and sex outside of marriage weren't even on the radar when I was a teenager.)

So I had the idea that being holy was about not doing wrong things, not sinning and avoiding doing certain things, rather than a rich and positive trait that is far more about being loving, pure and full of God's presence and power.

Peter has carefully explained the living hope and salvation that believers benefit from, and having established the truth of God's work in them, he goes on to press them to live accordingly. The tone changes from encouragement and teaching to command and exhortation.

As I grew in faith I wasn't always convinced that the teaching I was given to behave in a pure and honourable way was for my good. It is easy to regard such advice to be godly as restrictive or repressive. At times, it did seem that God might be a bit of a killjoy. I don't know whether it is the benefit of age and experience, but I recognize now that being holy, doing things God's way, is by far the best way to live. To live God's way in a holy and faithful manner is the best possible life, for us and for the first readers of this letter. Peter indicates a number of ways of being holy:

▶ Be alert – recognize that Christians face temptations and spiritual battles. Be aware of those areas that might be a weakness and might undermine faith and holiness.

▶ Be fully sober – be thoughtful and measured in what you do. Don't be carried away by excesses in drink, persuasive marketing or unhelpful influences. Be conscious of those influences that are destructive.

▶ Be full of hope in Christ – keep at the centre of your life that vision of Christ's return and his presence. How easy it is to be full of hope in the wrong things. Hope for that new job or new relationship. Hope in a pay rise or education. To be holy is to put our hope in Jesus Christ himself and him alone.

▶ Be obedient – obedience is not a popular concept to the twenty-first-century Western mind. People reserve the right to question and query. However, as children of the King of Kings, obedience is central to holiness. To obey is to be what God wants us to be, to do what he wants and to become more and more like him – obeying in all things, in the routine issues of honesty, integrity and the spiritual disciplines of prayer and giving.

To be holy is to be set apart from the corrupt and tainted things of this world. God is holy, for all that can be said about him is good, positive and pure. To be holy is to be like God; not just empty of anything corrupt, but full of life and love and all that is creative and good. To be holy is to be not only pure and virtuous; it is also to be faithful, loyal, loving, compassionate, generous and joyful.

As Peter writes, he quotes from Leviticus, an astonishing Old Testament book, which records God's law and reflects his holiness in broad and deep ways. God's holiness is expressed in the rules he gives for his people. These not only seek to maintain religious duties and worship which rightly honour God, but also regulate the community in a wholesome way. Even God's directions regarding the poor, the disabled, foreigners and families (Leviticus 19) emphasize his holy love and character.

God is described as holy and as Father and Judge. This might cause a tension for our limited understanding. How can God be loving and compassionate as a father, and judge impartially? The answer is that God can be perfect as Judge and Father because he is holy. His judgments are perfect, and it is only with Christ as Saviour that anyone can be declared innocent before him.

Peter reinforces his exhortation to live holy lives by appealing to the sacrificial death of Christ on the cross. Just as a lamb was sacrificed in Old Testament times to take the punishment for sin, so Jesus is the perfect sacrifice offering his life for the sins of humankind. Those who have been delivered from the punishment for sin by faith in Christ must live in recognition of the price that has been paid on their behalf. Reverent fear or awesome respect can be shown by behaving in a manner appropriate to those chosen by God.

The indication is that the readers were from ungodly

backgrounds (verse 18), which Peter describes as empty, not unlike so many lifestyles today. Their new life and freedom was not bought cheaply – nothing as common as gold and silver; it was the unique and precious blood of Christ on the cross that made their salvation possible. And this was not unplanned or spontaneous when things started to go wrong with the world, but God planned this before creation, knowing that the people he made would need to be forgiven.

**Questions**

1. How can holiness be presented to young people in such a way that it is seen as positive and fulfilling, and not boring?
2. What advice from Peter about holiness do you personally need to heed most?
3. Would the church receive greater respect today if its representatives showed greater evidence of holiness?

# 1 Peter 1:22 – 2:3

## The best diet for the born again

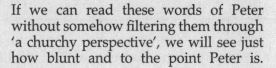

**Having become Christians and tasted of God's goodness, Peter encourages his readers to have a bigger appetite for the things of God and to encourage that appetite by right living.**

If we can read these words of Peter without somehow filtering them through 'a churchy perspective', we will see just how blunt and to the point Peter is.

Already in this letter he has spoken of the amazing hope that believers have and the salvation that belongs to them, and he has urged them to be holy because they will inherit all God's blessings for eternity. Now he presses them and us further.

Since disciples of Jesus Christ have been purified by being forgiven and by the cleansing work of the Holy Spirit, then they must follow that through with other actions. They have obeyed the call to be disciples of Jesus Christ; they have responded to the appeal to repent and turn to Christ, but there is more. God wishes to bless in even greater ways, and there are even deeper works that God wishes to do in transforming all of his people to be like himself. There are three ways in which God's people can co-operate with their Lord in order to go deeper with him.

1. Love one another deeply. We live in a particularly individualistic culture in the West and increasingly in other areas of the world. It is easy, if we are not careful, to individualize Christian faith and make it something that is just between us and God. Peter makes it clear that for all Christians the gospel has community repercussions. To be a Christian is not only to love God but also to love each other, genuinely, sincerely and deeply. And to love is to serve and walk with people, even when it is a struggle. It is to forgive and show compassion and care.

2. Get rid of destructive qualities such as deceit, spite and unpleasant talk. We sometimes have a rose-tinted view of the early church, thinking it must have been good to be part of a community before it became set in its ways, and before traditions became difficult to change. At times, there appears to have been an enviable freedom in New Testament communities, and yet the basic issues that create havoc in church life, that cause hurt and pain, were around in the first century, just as they are in the twenty-first century. How frequently church meetings and congregational forums have been

damaged by destructive and spiteful words. Ananias and Sapphira (Acts 5:1–11) are not the only Christians to have been deceitful, but possibly the only ones to have been punished quite so abruptly.

Peter is logical and reasonable. Since we have been saved, forgiven and made holy, we must live as if we have. We know we cannot deceive God, so why deceive others? We know that we dishonour God when we speak without love or concern or with spite, so we must not do it. God loves all his people and is faithful and generous to all, so there is no place for envy in God's community.

3. Thirst for God, drink of his presence, and so grow and be strong in Christ. As with any delicious, quenching drink, when we have tasted a little, we want more, and so it is with God's presence and power working in us – having tasted a little of it, this should create an appetite for far more. There should be a dissatisfaction with drinking only a little from all that God offers, and there should be an urgent desire to go deeper and know more of God's way and purposes.

It is easy in the rough-and-tumble of life to lose one's thirst for God. We replace it so easily with other things that satisfy for a while, but fail to give the spiritual food needed to be mature in faith and discipleship. Pure spiritual milk may come to us in different ways. It may be the milk of fellowship, worship and prayer that is the spiritual food your soul is missing, so you haven't grown in your faith because you are spiritually malnourished. It may be the milk of the Word of God that is lacking. Regular meals of the words and message of the Bible to strengthen, shape and mould your thinking and attitudes are essential. We are so easily influenced by things that are not godly or helpful, and if our spiritual diet lacks the basic nutrients, we will begin to show signs of spiritual ill health. Sailors used to get rickets and scurvy, because on long journeys overseas they didn't get vitamins C or D. Peter urges his readers and us to have a balanced spiritual diet in every way: loving others, getting rid of all those characteristics which are unworthy of God's people, and drinking of the rich milk of God's Word, presence, worship and community.

In verses 23–25, Peter explains why Christians should live differently as disciples of Jesus Christ. In their old life outside of Christ they were destined like grass and flowers to wither and die, but now they have been born again. They have heard and responded to the gospel message, the Word of God, and as part of God's purposes and plans, they will now live for ever. If this life is all there is, then living selfishly doesn't matter too much; survival of the fittest makes sense, but that is not the case. Christians know that this life is not all there is. We do not just wither and die at the end of physical life, but having been transformed by the Word of God, we will have an eternal existence.

This is the highest of all motivations for living in a godly way, in order to be ready for life fully with God and life for ever. We might as well get used to living that way now.

## Questions

1. How can individual believers increase their appetite for spiritual milk?
2. Should we be surprised and disappointed when deceit, hypocrisy, envy and slander appear in politics and the church? Is it not just a sign of fallen humanity?
3. Do people today acknowledge that their life is transient like grass, or are there ways in which people reveal that they hope to cheat death in some way?

---

**Peter teaches about the church as the community of God's people. Christians are described as 'living stones', built together on the foundation of the Living Stone, Jesus Christ.**

---

This passage is one of the most important sections on the church in the New Testament. You might also think this passage is an astonishing victory of optimism and hope over realism and disappointment. Was the church so much better in Peter's day than today, so that he could speak in such positive and affirming ways? Or was it that Peter saw the potential, possibilities and reality behind the problems, which enabled him to see what the church was being made into, despite the human issues that caused it to trip and fail?

Peter refers to a wide range of Old Testament images to make his argument about the community of God's people, the church. He sees the church following in continuity with God's people through all the Old Testament generations from Abraham, while being a new expression of what it means to be the people of God.

Many times in the Old Testament the stones of the temple were given great significance, and Peter picks up this idea and uses it of Christ himself, who is 'The Stone', the one living foundation on which all else is built. Christ is the Stone, precious to God, who brought about salvation. Those who have faith in Christ are also living stones being built together to make the church or a spiritual house, fulfilling all the Old Testament temple activities. Living stones are like the priests who have access to God, who offer worship to God and who offer spiritual sacrifices.

These spiritual sacrifices are not for sin, as Christ himself is the only one who could offer that sacrifice, but for offering praise and prayer and selfless acts as worship to God.

The church, as it is viewed around the world today, rarely has this glowing image. Rather than being a community made up of living stones, it seems to get dragged into power struggles or political wrangles that prevent it being the people of God. And yet despite all the ungodly activities that are represented as church, God maintains his community, his people and their living activities.

Peter quotes from Isaiah 28:16, Psalm 118:22 and Isaiah 8:14 to explain how the church can be the continuation of God's purposes and plans through Israel, even though many Jews rejected Jesus, and so many Gentiles fail to believe in him. God is creating a new spiritual temple, the foundation stone of which is Jesus, and all who trust in him become living stones and part of that holy community, the church. What many Jews spurned is the central feature of God's new covenant with his people. The feature that many stumble over is the crucial factor in God's community, Jesus.

For those Christians living in the first century, Peter explains why the church is not numerically larger. It is reasonable to wonder that if Jesus is the fulfilment of the Old Testament prophets, why are so many Jews not his followers, and if Jesus is such good news to Gentiles, why do so many not obey his teaching? The answer is that many Jews have rejected the Messiah, as they have rejected God's plans throughout history, and many Gentiles have found the Living Stone, Jesus, not a foundation to build their lives on and through which to find forgiveness, but a barrier or obstacle. In their pride or self-centredness, the Living Stone is a stumbling block, which they will not accept.

The conclusion of this passage (verses 9–10) is a clear statement of God's perspective on the church. As God's people work together as his community, they are the chosen people of God; they are a holy nation and a special people belonging to God. Echoing images from Isaiah and Hosea, Peter encourages us to understand that the purpose of God's community, the church, is to declare the praises of God and never to forget that we are the people who have received mercy and kindness from God.

In Peter's day as today, it is difficult to recognize the organization of the church and its denominations in these high ideals of community life, and yet this is what the church is to be. We are not to stand alone as Christians; when we come to faith, we are joined into a spiritual community where we are to play our part. We are to offer spiritual sacrifices, using our gifts and resources as our worship. Those who claim a relationship with God through Christ and yet never involve themselves in God's community would be unrecognized by the apostle Peter.

To belong to God is to belong to the people of God and his community. It is to be separate from the communities who focus only on this life and the material world, and it is to have the highest affirmation of being royal priests, holy citizens, special possessions of the Sovereign Lord.

For Peter's readers this was complete status reversal. In their communities, they were marginalized because of their social position. They were poor, with no social power or significance and few rights, and yet, in God's social structures they are children of the King; they are royalty, set apart from the rest as holy and sacred, and they are specially loved by God.

At times all of us need special encouragement. The world we live in grinds people down and makes them feel worthless; it discourages and creates despair. Even in the church people can be hurt and trampled on, but in God's community, those who have faith in Christ are affirmed in the highest ways.

### Questions

1. Peter speaks of the community of the church in the highest possible terms. Do you share his view of the church in the light of your experience of church life?

2. In what ways today do people stumble and fall because of Jesus Christ?
3. Peter suggests that all believers have a priestly function, offering prayers and worship to God. How can the 'priesthood of all believers' be recognized, while ordained ministry prevails in most denominations?

## What lies behind the letter of 1 Peter?

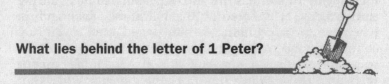

Peter wrote to Christian believers in the area known today as Turkey. They were small, scattered congregations or individual believers, struggling to continue in faith in an unsympathetic world. The named places (1:1) are five Roman provinces of the time.

Peter writes to a socially mixed readership, but mostly from the lower strata of society. His reference to slaves and not masters suggests that congregations were made up of the less powerful and wealthy, and the emphasis on wives may suggest that Peter is addressing more Christian women than men. While there appears to be a mixture of Jews and Gentiles, the signals from the letter are that converts from paganism are in the majority.

Peter may not have known the readers of his letter personally. It is possible he had not visited the area where they live and may have understood their plight only by receiving news of their circumstances from visitors to Rome, but he was able to identify with their situation from his own similar experiences.

There is an emphasis on suffering and coping as a Christian in the face of opposition. Peter writes to congregations facing harassment and pressure, if not outright persecution, which came a little later with the Emperor Nero. Still they were misunderstood and discouraged in their faith by those around them and those who had power and authority. It may be difficult for many Christians today to identify readily with the experiences being referred to. However, believers who are in situations of hostility and direct enmity with the gospel will find the words echo powerfully down the centuries. The focus on perseverance and maintaining a distinctive Christian lifestyle is important for all believers in all circumstances. For those who do not face the pressure of opposition the message of 1 Peter has much to say about understanding the realities of the world in which we live, and in preparing for opposition when it comes.

There has been some discussion about whether 1 Peter is a letter or really a sermon or a manual for church membership, or even a handbook preparing converts for baptism. Since the letter is not addressed specifically and appears so comprehensive, people have wondered if it was originally intended as a letter. There is much in the letter that indicates that it can be used as a basic handbook for Christian living. So, while Peter covers many themes that would be included in first-century discipleship courses, letters were an obvious way of communicating teaching and greetings, encouragement and inspiration. It is likely that Peter used material from different church contexts as he wrote his letter, which could be used for a variety of purposes within the receiving church groups.

# 1 Peter 2:11–17

Living within godless social structures

**The way Christians live in relation to their unbelieving neighbours or to human authority should reflect their priority of serving the aims of the kingdom of God.**

In the opening section of his letter, Peter has laid a clear foundation for his readers, reminding them of their salvation in Christ, their hope of eternity and their citizenship in God's holy community. In this section, he begins a new theme, going through to 4:11. Note the opening phrase, 'Dear Friends', here and 4:12, to introduce each part. The focus of this section is the relationship of Christians to various social institutions, and he begins by looking at how Christians should relate to the society in which they live and particularly to those in authority.

For Christians in any political context, the issue of accepting the authority of local or national government is not theoretical, but practical and problematic. Today there appears to be an increase in the use of authority that can threaten Christian values. For example, Christians in China might contravene authority by preaching, witnessing or holding a Bible study. Christians in Muslim countries might breach authority by denying the holiness of Muhammad, and in the UK, employment law might make it difficult for Christian employers to follow the requirement that a person working in a Christian organization need not follow Christian teaching in terms of sexual conduct. Furthermore, there are suggestions that teaching about the uniqueness of Christ could contravene laws involving tolerance and respect for other faiths in numerous contexts. While these may not be routine issues for all believers, maintaining godly values such as integrity, fairness and justice may impact the lives of Christians on an almost daily basis. In these verses Peter gives guidelines on how Christians should live when the culture is hostile to faith and Christ-centred lifestyles.

Peter acknowledges that the social context of those to whom he is writing is like a foreign land. Followers of Christ are citizens of God's kingdom, but Peter's readers find themselves temporarily resident in a society dominated by ungodly values. Living in a foreign culture meant they were misunderstood and misrepresented. They were accused of incest and cannibalism in some circles, and regarded as being communities of vice.

Just as today, the Christians Peter was writing to were surrounded by sexual permissiveness, material obsession and self-centredness. This is an alien culture for the people of God. Peter warns his readers to resist such temptations that damage their inner spiritual being, and to live lives of integrity so that others will be impressed. Then, even if they are accused of being intolerant or narrow-minded because of their Christian faith, they will be respected for their honourable way of life.

The curious little phrase, 'glorify God on the day he visits us' (verse 12), has Old Testament associations. It may refer to the Day of Judgment when all those who criticize Christians will recognize the truth of Christian beliefs. Alternatively, it may refer to God visiting by his Holy Spirit, so that the good works of believers lead to others coming to faith and praising God, and the example of Christians has opened their eyes to the truth of the gospel.

In verses 13–17, the idea of living good lives is unpacked further. What does it mean to live a godly life with regard to those who govern and have authority? Human authorities have their power in order to benefit society and are sanctioned by God himself. God gives power to those in command, so that wrongdoers are restrained and those who do good are affirmed. In other words, Peter suggests that Christians should be good citizens, living good lives, being respectful towards those who hold office, and honouring those who work hard for the community.

It follows that Christians should be willing to take office themselves or to serve the community in some political or official capacity, and in doing so, they will be commended for doing what is right and good. Christians are not to be isolationists who withdraw from the world and its needs; they are encouraged to play their part in being worthwhile community members, and so silencing the accusations of those who falsely accuse Christians.

Down the centuries, many Christians have taken civic or political office in order to fulfil their Christian responsibilities. It is a worthy path for a disciple of Christ, but it is fraught with the potential for compromise and the loss of integrity and Christlike character that Peter so strongly commends.

This teaching begs the question 'what is the Christian response if the authority is unjust or conflicts with Christians values?' My reply would be that we should obey and conform to the requirements of the state and human authority until it conflicts with our obedience to Christ and his service. Then our words can be as Peter's were in Acts 4:19: 'Judge for yourselves whether it is right in God's sight to obey you rather than God.' He goes on to imply that he feels compelled to do what God said.

It is easy to take a narrow, legalistic approach to obedience to God or state, and to make unwarranted claims to civil disobedience, justifying it as obedience to God. There are issues where it is unclear, but we need to obey the state as far as we are able, even when we don't agree with it , if it does not conflict directly with Christian truth.

And a final thought on 'submit yourselves for the Lord's sake to every human authority' (verse 13); note that it is not for the sake of a quiet life or to avoid drawing attention to yourself, but so that the purposes and plans of God's kingdom might be furthered. That is Peter's concern with all the teaching in this section – do whatever best serves the purposes of the kingdom of God.

## Questions

1. Think about why authority in principle is God's provision for society. What would be the effect if there were no authority? Is even unjust authority better than no authority?
2. How would you advise a believer to live as a witness for Christ in a country where it is illegal to proselytize?
3. Peter speaks of 'showing proper respect to everyone' (verse 17). Who would you include as those who should be respected? Are there any you could not respect?

# 1 Peter 2:18–25

## Injustice and Christ's example

**In the social context of slavery and injustice, Peter appeals to his readers to follow the example of Christ and serve the purposes of the kingdom of God.**

 It is almost impossible for the twenty-first-century mind to understand how the apostle Peter could seemingly acquiesce with injustice to such an extent that he commands slaves, 'submit to your masters with all respect, not only to those who are good and considerate but also to those who are harsh.' This would appear to be a tyrant's charter or a tormenter's authorization; what has this to do with the good news of Jesus Christ who came to 'release the oppressed' (Luke 4:18)?

As we seek to understand these words, we need to remember several things. First, Peter is writing to believers in Jesus Christ, who have a living hope of life beyond death, in eternity. This life is only a temporary state – what is more important is the life beyond, and so the difficulties of this life are to be seen as a prelude to something much greater and permanent. Secondly, he is writing to a congregation where slaves would have been a significant proportion of the community, and any action would need to reflect well on Christians and the gospel.

Peter is not sanctioning slavery; he is encouraging Christians to make the best possible personal response to injustice. Neither is he condoning slavery or the abuse of people in any context; he is giving advice to Christians on the best way to act when treated unfairly. Throughout the Bible, particularly in the words of the prophets, but also in the words of the law, it is clear that God's pattern for communities is that all people should be treated with respect and dignity, whatever their role in society. Peter's teaching here is not about our response on behalf of others when they are mistreated, but about dealing with issues for oneself.

Christians should work to promote the abolition of slavery in all its forms, but it is difficult to compare slavery in the twenty-first century with slavery in the first century. In Peter's time, slavery would for some have been no worse than being 'in service', and the notion of freedom to change jobs and travel would have been an alien concept. In many respects, the parallels are much more with employment and workers today. Since slavery is largely illegal in the twenty-first century, anyone trapped in a harsh regime today is likely to be treated in the most appalling ways. While slavery in the first century was a harsh and brutal regime for some, for others it was possibly no worse than being 'a wage slave' today.

Peter encourages his slave readers to show respect and to honour those with power over them, whether they treat them well or not. If they react commendably and endure harsh treatment because of their Christian faith, then that will be to their credit before God, but if they are punished for their own bad behaviour, then that has no merit in it at all.

Those who find themselves in unfair circumstances should follow the example of Christ himself. Peter makes the shocking statement that they are called to follow his example, and this may include suffering. Christ himself was sinless and without fault in any way, and yet he was violently abused, insulted and threatened. He did not retaliate or take revenge, but died a sacrifice for sin.

In these words about Christ, Peter offers an awesome model for discipleship as well as a powerful summary of the gospel. We are to accept that unfairness and injustice may come our way in life; we are not to retaliate or to take revenge. We are to hope and pray that our example might benefit our persecutor. This is similar to the teaching of Jesus in Matthew 5:39–40, when he said 'Do not resist an evil person. If someone strikes you on the right cheek, turn to him the other also. And if someone wants to sue you and take your tunic, let him have your cloak as well.'

At almost exactly the central place in the letter, Peter is readily distracted from ethical considerations to focus on the cross. In suggesting to the slave readers how they should live, he is reminded of the powerful imagery of the crucifixion, and briefly but profoundly takes the readers back to the central tenet of faith. In these few words he reflects on the imagery of Isaiah 53 of the innocent lamb taking the punishment for the sin of the world. The example of Christ is not to do with non-retaliation; but it is a positive example about trusting God to judge justly and fairly.

Peter cannot help but remind his readers of all that Christ has done for them. They have been healed by the willing suffering of Christ; they are forgiven because of his courage in pain; they are able to live godly lives because of his obedient submission to the purposes of God the Father.

The final verse of this section is a necessary reminder that slaves and free, powerful and weak, rich and poor are all similarly in need. All are like lost sheep until they are found by God and they turn to Jesus Christ the Shepherd. There is warmth and comfort in these words. Those enslaved and struggling with the burdens of life have a shepherd who is concerned for them, and who protects and keeps their inner being and understands their pain.

## Questions

1. How might a Christian worker in an unjust employment situation apply Peter's words to his/her context?
2. What should be the church's response to slavery around the world in the twenty-first century?
3. Reflect on Peter's words about Christ in verses 21–25. What new insight or important truth does it bring to mind?

## Stop and look: Slavery

Peter's teaching to slaves in his first letter in the first century is shocking to a twenty-first-century mind. Today, when slavery is illegal in almost every country of the globe, Peter's words appear to be an oppressor's charter or an ultra-right-wing manifesto. How can we understand his teaching and make sense of his advice when the social context was so different? Do Peter's words to slaves have any relevance to people today?

Peter's teaching here can be helpful for twenty-first-century Christians, if we recognize the completely different social framework, and seek to grasp the underlying principles . At the time Peter was writing this letter, there were millions of slaves in the Roman Empire, and people were slaves for different reasons. Some were born into slavery; some were enslaved because of debt or as prisoners or war. Some slaves were reasonably well treated and some were dealt with appallingly – oppressed, abused and dishonoured.

Although he is aware of the difficulties of those in

slavery, Peter's focus is the kingdom of God and bringing in the new age of the rule of God when all will be set free, spiritually and socially. Peter's concern is that all energies and actions should be geared towards the kingdom of God, and so he might have seen a campaign to free slaves as a distraction to the main work of telling people about the gospel.

Peter thought that Jesus would return soon, certainly within the lifetime of many of the slaves to whom he wrote, and his primary motivation was the spiritual revolution offered by the gospel, which would impact society in the deepest of ways. He wanted all Christians, both slaves and free people, to live in such a way that maximized fruitfulness for the kingdom of God.

Peter emphasizes that any relationship brings with it responsibilities. Whether these relationships are with Christians or non-Christians, at work, home or leisure, the issue should be 'how can I best live for God in this relationship?' And linked to that is 'how can this relationship best reflect the gospel?' In the social context of the day, Peter's judgment was that personal retaliation for being a slave or for receiving injustice as a slave would not have been appropriate. It would not have benefited the gospel. Therefore, Peter says that slaves should accept injustice, unfair as it is, and use it as an opportunity to bring glory to God.

This is not to say that Christians are in favour of slavery – of course not. Paul encourages slaves to gain their freedom if they can (1 Corinthians 7:21), and the words of the prophets such as Amos encourage believers to strive for justice and humanity in all societies as a working out of God's purposes for his community. Peter and Paul would recognize that social transformation is a crucial aspect of the gospel; Jesus was concerned to teach about feeding the hungry, releasing the captives and clothing the naked. The apostles, however, would have seen this social transformation as possible only when there was a transformation of the spiritual life of the community. Without the gospel's liberating effect then social justice can never be more than incomplete or an empty hope. Slavery would end only when the spiritual impetus of the gospel was at the heart of the vision for freedom. And so it happened in the nineteenth century when William Wilberforce was motivated by the love of Christ to free slaves and campaign against slavery.

Those who think that Peter has sold out to the establishment and supports the status quo of the rich suppressing the weak have not understood the gospel imperative or the first-century context. At the heart of the gospel is status reversal, when slaves become free people, the weak become strong and the poor become rich. With this in mind, Peter has a much greater agenda than the abolition of slavery, his vision is the abolition of sin and death, which is what is needed for the whole of humankind. Slaves may be released from captivity only to find they are still held captive by sin. Peter is concerned for the greater freedom of life and spirit that all might receive through Jesus Christ.

For twenty-first-century slaves the social context has completely changed, and while the principle of doing whatever is best for furthering the kingdom of God remains the same, the practice of personally accepting illegal and unjust slavery is not. In a culture where slavery is illegal, it is in the interests of Christian slaves to do all they can to receive justice.

# 1 Peter 3:1–7

## Marriage and Christian faith

**Wives are to honour their husbands as required by the culture of the day, in order to further the kingdom of God. Husbands are to respect and honour their wives as partners in Christ.**

I feel as if I need to take a deep breath and, more importantly, pray fervently as we consider these words. A woman writer saying that Peter doesn't mean what we think he means – she would say that! I hope for a moment we can try to set aside our prejudices, and come to these words over which many battles have been fought, and find God's truth so that all men and women within our Christian communities might be served, but then I am as much a product of prejudices as anyone else. So perhaps we will come openly and honestly to these words, and pray for clarity and understanding as we work through controversial issues.

Just as slaves (2:13–20) were to submit to unfair masters, and Jesus submitted to an unjust death on the cross (2:21–25), so wives must be willing to submit to husbands as was demanded by the prevailing culture, and particularly they must submit to unbelieving husbands.

Imagine a Muslim woman converting to the Christian faith – what is the most helpful advice her pastor could give her? Be a good wife, love your husband, honour and respect him and submit to him, and in so doing he will not be threatened by your faith in Christ. He might even see it as a good thing and come to faith himself.

Christian wives have a responsibility to be the best possible wives – to love and cherish, to comfort and respect, not to abdicate their responsibilities in marriage because they have found faith. They are commanded as married women to make a priority of supporting and caring for their husband and family. Please note that these verses refer to families and marriage relationships; they do not refer to wider community issues. They have no significance for men and women in general, or men and women in the workplace or in church leadership. Their primary aim is to teach that wives should not become a hindrance to their husbands and others coming to faith because their behaviour within marriage shocks and upsets.

Today it would mean that wives should respect their husbands and love them. This will mean different things for different marriage relationships. No couple relates in the same way as another or has the same expectations or assumptions, but, as servants of Christ and children of the King of Kings, wives must do all they can to reflect godliness in their marriage, to honour their marriage vows and to maintain a rich and full marriage relationship.

Christian wives are encouraged to think beyond the superficial and decorative. Their beauty is to be more to do with character and behaviour than with decoration and dress. This is a useful reminder to both women and men today. So much emphasis is placed on image and appearance that even in church communities it can be destructive and unhelpful. Clearly, in Peter's time there were fashions as there are today for different hairstyles, jewellery and clothing, and these could be harmless or they could be damaging if too much importance is attached to outward appearance.

Feminist theologians and women's rights writers have had a field day with verses 1 and 4 of this passage. They appear to reinforce an oppressive view of women, which, they would argue, is characteristic of biblical teaching. But I would say that the Bible is good news for women – the best news even, and these thoughts of Peter need to be understood in the context of the day in which they were written, and interpreted for today.

Today women are rightly encouraged to use their full

range of gifts, abilities and talents in their career, family and community life. The 'unfading beauty of a gentle and quiet spirit' of which Peter speaks would not be recognized as a priority quality in women, and to encourage women to reflect such character would be regarded as yet another attempt to repress them, to keep them in their place and not allow them their full place in society.

So how are we to understand Peter today? Against the background of a male-dominated society as it had been for centuries, wives were being taught not to do anything that would hinder the spread of the gospel. If that meant at times submitting like slaves, then that was a small price to pay for all the benefits of being saved. Furthermore, wives should seek to cultivate the kind of character that would best reflect the gospel within the community; in other words, to be women of good character and rely on inner beauty, rather than outward decoration.

My understanding is that the cultural background of this passage reflects that women in the first century did not enjoy the rights or power of women in the twenty-first century. It would therefore have been inappropriate and inadvisable for Christian women of Peter's day to demand equality, and to become assertive and dominant, which would hinder rather than advance the gospel.

Maybe today, women who are wives should recognize their responsibility not just to forge ahead with a career, without consideration for their husband. Good character demands that marriage vows are maintained honestly and with determination to build a good relationship at all times.

If all this seems a little hard on the women, then Peter is also concerned to make clear his high expectations for husbands in Christian marriage. Husbands are instructed to treat their wives with respect; this was a radical counter-cultural obligation. Wives were the possession of their husbands, and some husbands would consider themselves well within their rights to do as they pleased as far as their wives were concerned. Again the focus is on doing whatever will further God's purposes and plans.

Treat your wives as partners in the salvation given
through Jesus Christ, and live so that nothing will stop
your prayers for godliness and God's purposes being
fulfilled.

## Questions

1. Do you think Peter's teaching is unfair to Christian
   wives?
2. How would Peter adapt his teaching to make it relevant
   to Christian wives today?
3. Is Peter responsible in part for the oppression of women
   within the church over the past 2000 years, or is it the
   responsibility of those who misunderstand biblical
   teaching in order to make women submissive?

## Is Peter unfair to women?

Many who hold to a feminist view find the Bible insuffer-
ably male, and highlight Peter's words in 3:1–6 as evidence
of a male-dominated gospel message that is not good news
for women. This is difficult for those of us who believe that
the Bible is good news for everyone, particularly women,
and to seek to understand some of the seemingly oppressive passages does require careful reflection.

Passages such as 1 Timothy 2:11–15 do require careful
study to make sense of the meaning and to interpret the
gospel of Jesus as good news for everyone. In this passage
in Peter's letter, it is apparent that his focus is not on
women in leadership, marriage or ministry. His concern is
that Christians living in an unsympathetic context, such as
marriage to a non-believer and in a male-dominated
culture as it was in Peter's day, should do all they can to
promote the gospel.

As with slaves, Peter is concerned for wives to use their

freedom in Christ appropriately and not break the cultural norms of the day, as such behaviour would undermine the mission aims of the Christian community. While many commentators and interpreters have taken these words as being unfair to women, Peter is encouraging a radically new respect for wives in marriages that strengthened their position and their role.

I would suggest that this passage is fair to women for a number of reasons:

1. It is written to wives and not to women in general, and should not be interpreted more widely.

2. Wives are being asked to show the kind of character that reflects the person of Christ. They are not to rely on the outward appearance of gold or clothing. Today these words might equally apply to men. The emphasis is that both women and men have the privilege of belonging to and being loved by Christ, and this brings a dignity and respect that should be reflected in Christlike behaviour.

3. Peter encourages Christian husbands to love their wives and show them respect and honour. In the culture of the day this was a reversal of norms, but it was the pattern most likely to attract an unbelieving wife to faith or sustain a believing wife as a Christian.

4. The 'weaker partner' is surely unfair to wives? Wives are not weaker; many show strength of character and emotion, spiritual strength and leadership strength that might put their husbands to shame. However, maybe Peter is not making a point about different kinds of strength, but recognizing that physically most husbands are stronger than their wives and ought to take responsibility for physically strenuous duties, and not leave them to women all the time. If added to this we recognize that many wives would be pregnant or caring for young babies a significant amount of time, this would add to the argument that wives may need support when they are physically vulnerable.

5. In his day, Peter was being fair to wives and women in the church whose first priority was the kingdom of God. Writers down the centuries have misunderstood Peter, and made him appear unfair for women today. They have taken Peter's idea of 'weaker partner' and used it to argue that women are weaker intellectually or emotionally.

# 1 Peter 3:8–16

Godly common sense and good living

**Simple advice about how to live at peace with fellow believers and unsympathetic neighbours.**

Having addressed wives and husbands, Peter spreads his net wider and speaks to everyone about how to live together in ways that honour God. He gives  simple instructions that are a reminder to all of how to live in a community, whether this is a family unit or a church community.

▶ *Be like-minded* – aim to see things in the same way, with Christ at the centre and with his values shaping all thoughts and attitudes. This does not mean there is no room for creative disagreement, discussion or debate, but strive for unity and understanding each other, in order that progress can be made for God's kingdom.

▶ *Be sympathetic* – how easy it is to criticize and back-bite without understanding people's circumstances. Peter encourages his readers to be sympathetic when things go wrong or relationships are tense; to be supportive of each other and seek to understand the situation rather than condemn. We never know the whole story of someone's circumstances; love always believes the best and therefore there is always room for sympathy.

▶ *Love one another* – how often this theme occurs in the teaching of Jesus and in the letters of the apostles. It is the foundation attitude of one believer to another, and yet all Christians need reminding of it again and again. How frequently God's people are unloving and malicious – this is destructive for the individual and for the community.

▶ *Be compassionate* – if being sympathetic is to seek to understand people's actions and circumstances, being compassionate is to show practical and active care and consideration. Both are an expression of love. To be sympathetic is to show love in words and understanding, and to be compassionate is to show love by helpful and kind behaviour.

▶ *Be humble* – in a world where we are encouraged to be assertive, and arrogance and pride are almost virtues, this particular instruction hits like a sledge-hammer. 'Be humble.' In other words, don't think of yourself as better than others. But I hear you saying 'I am more educated, more gifted and more experienced; is it not unrealistic, even hypocritical, to pretend others are better than I am?' To be humble is to acknowledge that opportunities, gifts and experience have been given, but to recognize all are from God and that he is the source of strength and any advantage. This does not make one person better than another, but requires humility to recognize that all we are is from God and without his grace we are weak and flawed before him.

▶ *Repay evil with blessing* – the desire for revenge is such a nasty issue. As I write, news is breaking of the shocking events in Lancaster County USA, where a bitter, vengeful man harbouring hurt and the desire for revenge for twenty years killed little innocent Amish girls in their schoolroom. While such events are thankfully rare, we should recognize the danger of holding on to resentment and anger. The teaching of Jesus echoed here by Peter is to respond to evil in whatever its form with goodness and love. That is impossible to do of ourselves. Our inclination is to retaliate, but with God's grace we can repay hatred and wrongdoing with love and good, and it is the best way forward for all communities.

▶ *Keep your tongue from evil* – the old saying 'if you can't think of anything good to say, then don't say anything at all' is not a bad paraphrase of Peter's thoughts. Words are so powerful in their effect. To have good relationships with people involves keeping your tongue under control and allowing only godly words from your mouth.

▶ *Seek peace and pursue it* – in relationships aim for harmony and peace: not peace at any price, not accepting wrong and evil, but finding a peaceful and constructive way of dealing with contentious situations. So easily people respond with suspicion and aggression these days; Peter's words to be always looking for a peaceful way forward are helpful in many circumstances of life.

Peter makes the reasonable comment that if you behave impressively before others with gracious acts and loving concern, then who will seek to harm you? Often people will be hostile if we give them a reason for being so, but if we are seen to be good and wholesome, then it will reduce mistrust and antagonism and give more opportunities for the work of the kingdom of God. In our zeal for faith, it is so easy to act ungraciously or even with arrogance; the words here remind us of the unhelpfulness of such an approach to all involved.

### Strategy for evangelism (verses 15–16)

Nestled into this section about maintaining good relationships with employers, in the home, and with authorities and people of the community, Peter gives a simple strategy for reaching out to others and for maintaining a godly lifestyle. He reminds us always to keep Christ at the centre of all that we are and all that we do. We cannot go far wrong when we hold on to that truth. So easily in our use of leisure time or in our ambitions and priorities we fail to acknowledge the presence of Christ and the necessity of letting his purposes mould and shape us.

When we live Christ-centred lives, it will inevitably lead to questions from others and comments about why we live as we do. When this happens, we must be ready to explain to people why we believe in Jesus; what our faith means to us and the difference our salvation makes. We do not need to be educated theologians; we do not have to know all the answers to people's questions, but we should be able to respond to any comment or enquiry with our story of faith – what God has done in our lives. We are encouraged to do this with gentleness and respect towards the person who asks; how often our witness has been smug and pompous or lacking confidence and gentle respect. If we live in such a way, ready and able to give an answer to others, then anyone who speaks against us will be ashamed, knowing that their criticism is unfounded.

### Questions

1. Remind yourself of occasions when your tongue has spoken evil or ungodly words. How can you avoid repeating this?
2. What evangelistic strategy has your church used recently? Does it conform to the words of Peter in verses 15–16?
3. If evil were repaid with blessing in the realm of global

politics, would it result in greater peace or greater oppression?

# 1 Peter 3:17–22
## The power of Christ's suffering

**The suffering of Christ is a model of how his followers should view suffering. Christ's suffering was unique as it brought forgiveness and reconciliation with God the Father.**

Many Christians have such a comfortable life and such high expectations of how their lives should work out materially and in terms of physical comfort,  that any low level of inconvenience is seen as suffering. In London, the Mayor introduced a congestion charge for those who take their car into the city during the day. Some Christians who objected to this charge regard it as suffering, because they have to pay to drive, find alternative routes to work or change their daily routine. Those of us who have such a view of suffering need a reality check.

As I write, I am in a refugee camp in Thailand on the border with Burma, where infant mortality is very high; women giving birth have severe complications and little medical care, and treatment for any special needs is extremely limited. The Karen people who largely populate this camp have no homeland; they cannot stay in Burma where they have lived for centuries, because they are attacked by the Burmese military, but neither can they travel in Thailand, for they have no rights in that country. They live on refugee rations and are confined in an area about five miles long by half a mile wide. Some have been there for sixteen years. When we look at the deep suffering of others, we begin to grasp that suffering may be a lot more than what we are facing.

Peter writes that if Christians suffer it should be for being holy, doing good and being faithful to Christ, not because of criminal activity or because they are an irritation to others. I think that very few Western Christians suffer for doing good. We live in such a tolerant and inclusive culture with protection of rights and freedom, that suffering is rarely our experience, but maybe also we are not suffering because we are not adequately pursuing the kingdom of God.

Christ suffered because he perfectly pursued the aims of the kingdom of God. His goodness challenged the unjust and ungodly power roles of the day. This reminder of Christ's suffering and his crucifixion leads Peter to talk about faith and the atoning effect of Christ's suffering. These verses come at the centre of the letter and are an awesome declaration of the work of Christ. A number of important points are made:

1. Jesus died *once* for sins. Peter emphasizes that the sacrifice of Jesus was perfect – once was enough. A perfect life for the sin of humankind. No longer were sheep to be slaughtered in the temple or goats offered for atonement. The one sacrifice for the whole of eternity was enough.

2. Jesus died the righteous for the unrighteous. Jesus was sinless, perfect, good in every way, and he gave his life for people who are all flawed, weak and unrighteous. It is becoming less popular in twenty-first-century culture to regard people as 'sinners'; somehow failure can be explained through upbringing, genes or other factors. This takes away from the biblical truth that all people, however good they might be, are unrighteous, bad before God, and they need a perfect sacrifice to put them right with God.

3. Jesus died to reconcile humanity to God. Before the death of Christ, the gulf caused by sin could not be

bridged. Sacrifices brought some forgiveness, but it was temporary and inadequate. The sacrifice had to be offered again and again. Only in Christ is peace with God made a permanent reality for those who believe.

4. Jesus died in the body – it was a genuine, physical death of the most horrible kind. Jesus did not swoon and then come round and not really die, as some have claimed. His life was extinguished. It was God's Spirit working that raised him to life. Death was conquered and God was victorious over sin and death.

The reference to imprisoned spirits, Noah and baptism is complex, and not a theme that is repeated elsewhere in the Bible. Scholars have researched and theorized about these verses, and the debate has focused on four basic issues: *when* Jesus preached; *where* Jesus preached; *to whom* he preached; and *the content* of his preaching. Did Jesus preach between his death and resurrection, or after the resurrection? The language of preaching by the Holy Spirit (verse 19) could refer to Jesus just before the resurrection or it could also mean a time after the resurrection. Both interpretations are possible.

Where did Jesus go to preach to the imprisoned spirits? This could refer to Hades, as mentioned in Isaiah 14:15, or going up to heaven, as discussed in Paul's writings (see 2 Corinthians 12:2). In either case, the direction is metaphorical; the words are intended to show that Jesus went to other spiritual realms as part of his work.

Then there is the question of whom Jesus was preaching to. Were they supernatural beings such as angels who had fallen (see Hebrews 12:9), or spirits of dead people or the disobedient souls of Noah's time, and was the disobedience actually disbelief or was it pride, arrogance or rebellion?

We also need to consider what Jesus preached – the content of his communication. It could be that he proclaimed that salvation had come, or perhaps he preached to condemn his hearers, or to give them a second opportunity for repentance.

We cannot be certain about these issues but the implication is that Jesus, through his death and resurrection, restrained the powers of evil. The illustration from Noah and from preaching to those who have neglected God's purposes, whether they are human or supernatural, is a reminder that those Christians who struggle with difficulties need not fear, for God is all-powerful and can protect them. His mention of water that saves is a reference to baptism, a symbol of salvation when someone has responded to God and has a clear conscience before him through faith in Jesus Christ.

## Questions

1. Since the suffering of Christ brought about such positive consequences, does that help us understand that our suffering may in a lesser way be a good thing?
2. What do you think happens to people when they die? What help are Peter's words in these verses in understanding life after death?
3. Reflect on the suffering of Christ and the pain he faced carrying the burden of humanity's sin. What response does this reflection provoke?

# 1 Peter 4:1–11

## Living in a pleasure obsessed world

---

**Christians brought out of a life of self-indulgence and pleasure seeking must not be tempted to slip back into old ways but should pursue discipleship in prayer, love and by using their gifts.**

---

On a staffroom notice board I remember seeing the sign 'You're born, you work, you die – so party while you have the chance.' This summarizes the view of  life of many without a Christ-centred or spiritual dimension to their life. Peter writes to people living amongst those with a similar hedonistic attitude. He lists the activities that such a godless life leads to: corruption, lust, drunkenness, extravagant indulgence of all kinds and reckless pleasure seeking. It could be a list describing every night of the weekend in the cities of the UK. People seem to enjoy being immoderate and making pleasure an idol.

Throughout his letter Peter has been teaching his readers to live as Christians in a hostile environment. In this part of his letter, he continues the theme of how God's people can live Christlike lives in a world that has different values. In this respect, things have not changed much over the centuries. God's people still find themselves in social environments where they are not comfortable or at home, and wonder how they should live.

Peter's advice is clear and uncompromising, and not necessarily comfortable reading. Christians must not return to their old lifestyles where the idols of drink, sex and indulgence were readily followed. God's people must live their lives in a God-centred way, not a human-centred way. They should accept that just as Christ committed himself to living only in holy ways and fulfilling his Father's plans, which meant accepting suffering, so disciples of Jesus should be willing to suffer in order to live Christlike lives.

Those who have put Christ at the centre will not have material pleasures and sensual experience as their focus, but their aim will be to fulfil the will of God. This may involve suffering, but that is a price worth paying for the pleasure of pleasing God. Curiously, Peter makes the comment that those who have suffered in the body have finished with sin. Certainly there are those who suffer and show no evidence of being sinless: in fact, their suffering may increase their sin as they become resentful and self-pitying. However, those who willingly suffer for the sake of Christ can learn the secret of putting God first, and therefore any temptation to sin is more easily resisted because they have broken the hold of sin in their lives.

I used to think that when I reached a certain age of maturity I would become godly, and many of the spiritual battles with sin would have been won. What I find is that the older and possibly more mature I get (I will let others be the judge), the battle with sin deepens. I am frustrated regularly that I have not finished with sin; I wish that I had. I seek desperately to live my life centred on the will of God, but I fail far more than I willingly admit. Peter may have in mind some state of sanctity or sainthood that some can achieve, and I have to admit I have known saintly Christians who do seem to have finished with sin – it is just that I haven't got there yet.

The world many of us live in is full of attractive, sinful activities that God's people should have left behind. Those who lay up their treasures on earth or who live for pleasure are often surprised and critical that we do not share their pursuits. At times, it can be quite a pressure to be working and living alongside those with such a material focus; they may be critical and mocking of a godly lifestyle, but we are called to be true to the values and behaviour of the kingdom of God. Even if people are abusive and bullying, Christians should seek to stay faithful to their Lord. Those who live self-centred lives will have to give account to God for their behaviour and attitudes, and they will be judged by their Maker for all they have done.

In verse 6 Peter picks up the theme of preaching to the dead, already mentioned in 3:19–20. Unclear as we are of the precise meaning, it does remind us that God's work continues beyond death and is a sharp reminder that death is not the end, and people will have to face God even if they have avoided him during their life on earth.

Peter continues this part of the letter with an encouragement to his readers to remain focused and clear thinking, so that they may pray and be ready for the return of Christ. The early church lived with a vivid expectation of the return of Christ and looked forward to the second coming in a matter of decades, not centuries. Peter's comment 'the end is near' is not mistaken despite the fact that for two millennia the church has waited and expected the end. In every generation the end could come; it is always near and runs parallel to this present age at all times. Since the first century, the church has been the poorer because it has lost a sense of urgency that Jesus is returning. We have all become a little cynical of the placard holder who has the words 'the end is nigh' for all to see in the town centre, but we should not be so dismissive of such reminders.

In verses 7–11 Peter gives advice relevant for the first or the twenty-first century, since the end is always close at hand. Do not get so caught up with things that you forget to pray and love each other deeply. Love does disguise and conceal sin and weakness in relationships and in a community. When people commit themselves to loving each other, many failings can be overlooked; many difficulties can be forgotten and love can find a way of bridging gulfs between people, whether those gulfs are caused by personality difficulties or differences in perspective and culture.

In the Western church we think we have the luxury of

falling out over minute doctrinal differences, but when we do fall out, our mission is undermined and the building of God's kingdom is halted. We need to recognize that what we share is much greater than that which divides us, and by loving and holding on to what is agreed, we should move forward with God's work.

Peter encourages hospitality – to be welcoming and offer food and drink to visitors. One bright spark has suggested that hospitality is 'making people feel at home when you wish they were at home'.

Peter is also concerned that his readers use the gifts God has given willingly and to the glory of God. Christians don't quite seem to understand that they are given gifts for the building up of the church, and not for the building up of their own reputation. God gives gifts for his purposes, and each one of us should use our gift willingly, humbly and conscientiously.

## Questions

1. How can there be a connection between suffering and 'being finished with sin'? Think of any examples of people who might help you understand this possibility.
2. In what ways can the church present the  gospel calling to live pure lives without appearing boring or a killjoy?
3. What spiritual gifts do you think are most missing from today's church?

# 1 Peter 4:12–19

## Chosen for the narrow path

---

**Christians should not be surprised when they face suffering. If believers suffer for their faith, then they share in the suffering of Christ and are drawn closer to him.**

---

As Peter again addresses the issue of tough times for Christians, he might have had in mind the words of Jesus that 'small is the gate and narrow the road  that leads to life' (Matthew 7:14). The path to the kingdom of God may not be as easy and straightforward as the road to destruction. It might pass through difficult times of challenge, but it is the path to eternity.

About four years ago, we had a holiday in Wengen in the Swiss Alps. It was the most wonderful place for walking, but we had our ten-year-old son with us and he enjoys running, cycling, in fact any sport, but not walking. We decided to take the cable car to the top of the mountain ridge and then walk back down – an hour's walk at the most. It was a beautiful summer's day, but after just 200 metres we realized this was not quite the casual afternoon stroll that we thought it was going to be. The path was very narrow; in places there was a sheer drop of several hundred feet and elsewhere the path had been washed away and all that was left was a shingle area, and crossing it with only our trainers on was treacherous.

About half way down we met a group of mountaineers dressed in full climbing gear; we felt under-prepared and underdressed. Eventually after two and a half hours we got to the outskirts of the village. The stress on our previously underutilized knee joints, and coping with a son who reminded his parents regularly that the one hour we had promised was now two and a half times that length did not make it even close to a gentle stroll. When we were nearly to the point of safety and comfort, I stepped on an innocent looking rock that was slightly damp and slippery, and went straight down. What looked like a pleasant stroll downhill all the way turned out to be a demanding and not altogether enjoyable ordeal.

Now think about the Christian life – it looks as though it should be easy. We are all loved by God and have his grace and his peace – so why is it that being a Christian, instead of being a pleasant afternoon stroll, is a mountain hike that threatens life and limb at every turn? Did Peter's readers feel this way?

Peter tells them not to be surprised that the Christian life is more demanding than they expected. Of course it didn't look difficult to begin with, but up close you realize the potential traps and dangers. It is not strange or exceptional that God's people should face tough times. Jesus faced tough times – his ministry was a battle, and similarly we are part of that battle and so his people will face tough times. Be glad that you share in the sufferings of Christ. Be glad that you begin to understand what it is to be God: to be holy and good and to face difficulties because of people who reject the best way to live.

Peter's readers were surprised that they were suffering. They knew people suffered for doing wrong, but suffering for doing right? – you would think God would step in and sort things out fairly. And the fact is that God does step in, but his time scale is so different from ours. God will transform situations, maybe not right now, but at some future time.

This letter was written about AD 64 and so it is unlikely that the large-scale public persecutions of Nero had begun. It is much more likely that the persecution the Christians were facing was localized: being falsely accused, ostracized or harassed. It may have been caused by rumours, local upsets and misunderstandings of which there were many.

If we are living as salt and light, then we will stir things up and difficulties will come our way. If we are salt, then we might not like to collude in slightly dishonest practices at work; or in gossip with the neighbours; or in drunken bouts with friends. Some might find us a little awkward. Be glad, find joy in difficulties, not because we are masochists and enjoy the pain, but because suffering brings us closer to the example of Christ. If we can recognize that suffering is part of this age, of the kingdom of God breaking in, then we can see that there is a purpose to it, and we can have joy because our suffering points to the glory of God's plans for eternity. We cannot share in Jesus' sufferings because they were unique. None of us can share in Jesus' actions and sacrifice, for he is the perfect Son of God, and yet we can share in his attitude and in his servanthood. We can 'leap for joy' in suffering, not because suffering is enjoyable, but because we are drawn closer to Jesus through it and our delight will be multiplied when we see what suffering has achieved.

## Don't suffer for doing wrong (verse 15)

If someone suffers because of their evil and wilful attitudes, there is no cause for joy. It is a sad and heart-breaking eventuality. Evil and wilful actions have consequences and punishments. If we suffer because we are in the wrong, if we have broken the law and been found out, there is nothing to be glad about. The best we can do is admit our failure, take the consequences, face the music and learn from it. If you have done wrong, don't try to wriggle out of it. Face up to it; pay the price.

## Questions

1. Many Christians around the world suffer for their faith and are persecuted. How does Peter suggest they view their suffering?
2. How can a Christian reconcile God's love and power with the fact of suffering in the world? Surely if he were

loving he would want to stop the suffering, and if he were powerful he could stop the suffering.

3. Is the church weakened because in many contexts it does not face opposition or suffering?

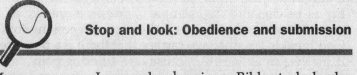

### Stop and look: Obedience and submission

Many years ago I remember hearing a Bible study leader introduce Peter's first letter with the words 'it is all about obedience'. I wasn't sure how far his interpretation arose from a personal agenda, since he used the letter to teach his listeners that we should obey him and all the other leaders, without question, in the organization where we were on a short-term placement.

Peter does speak about submission and obedience a number of times in this letter and we need to understand why he does so. It might then avoid an abuse of God's Word to bolster an unjustly autocratic leadership style.

In 1:1 and 1:14 Peter speaks of obedience to Jesus Christ. In 1:22 he speaks of obedience to the truth, and in 2:8 stumbling is the consequence of disobedience to the gospel message. Similarly 4:17 refers to judgment on those who do not obey the gospel of God. In 2:13 Peter speaks of obeying or submitting to human authorities, and in 2:18 slaves are taught to obey their masters, even if they are harsh and unjust. Similarly, wives are to be submissive to their husbands (3:1), and young people are encouraged to obey their elders (5:5).

Let me first explain what Peter intended when he wrote about obedience and submission. Let us then consider what implications his teaching has for us today as God's people. The background to this letter as with much of the New Testament is of people finding faith and freedom in Christ. Their new found freedom from sin and the discovery that they are significant before God in ways they had never before dreamed was an intoxicating combination. The danger was that they would take their Christian freedom and newly found self-worth in Christ and create social tensions and problems. This is particularly problematic for the people to whom Peter writes, who on the whole were the socially marginalized – slaves, women, poor and powerless. Their understanding of their citizenship of heaven and status as royal priests is causing them to question whether they need to continue to obey the government, employers or leaders. Furthermore, Christian slaves were empowered to think that they were no longer required to obey their masters, particularly if they were unjust and harsh, and Christian wives married to unbelieving husbands may have considered living more independently instead of following the social norm of submitting to their husbands.

It is hard for us in a twenty-first-century culture to understand the potential social effects of the gospel. It gave downtrodden individuals esteem and value that they had previously been denied by the social structures of the day. This was right and part of the blessings of the good news of Jesus Christ. However, Peter is concerned that the freedom and blessing that the believers have received might be wrongly used and might impede the progress of the kingdom of God. He encourages his readers to obey and submit in any situation where it might help the growth of the kingdom of God. Slaves and wives were to submit because that was their best opportunity of turning unbelieving masters and husbands to God. Younger people were to obey out of respect and in order to honour those senior in years, and to avoid some of the excess of enthusiasm that idealist youth may be prone to. The other references to obedience are to do with being obedient to Christ and the gospel, which is the only way to live with integrity as a Christian.

It is worrying when people see the word 'obedience' and are delighted because it gives them a stick with which to demand acquiescence. Peter advocates a respectful submission to those with authority, not a blind acceptance of authority under any circumstances. He himself made the point before the Sanhedrin when he was told not to preach that it is right to obey God rather than human authority (Acts 4:19–20).

Hence, Peter is not advocating an irresponsible obedience to those who have authority. We each have our own responsibility before God for our actions. As far as we are able we should use every relationship as an opportunity to reflect the example of Christ, and we should be prepared to model humility and holiness through submission and obedience, but we should also seek to defend those who are unjustly treated and be courageous in challenging authority when it is abused.

We live in a much less submissive age than previous generations, and Peter's teaching may not rest easily with our independent and assertive minds. We should be careful that our independence is not a cover for disobedience to the  gospel or a disguise for reinterpreting the Word of God so it is more palatable to our self-serving culture. There is a place for submission, and that should be a personal response to circumstances where it is deemed beneficial for the  gospel. However, those in positions of leadership within the church should not use such teaching to demand submission from others. Respect should be earned, and gracious leadership will receive the response it deserves without resorting to demands for obedience.

# 1 Peter 5:1–7

## Leadership in the church

---

**Those who lead the church receive guidance on using their position effectively for the sake of the kingdom of God. Advice is also given to the young and to those who worry.**

---

The temptation for all who find themselves in a leadership position is to enjoy their role and influence a little too much – to think of themselves as more important than those they are serving and to forget that the Lord is their master. Peter's words suggest that this may have been an issue in the churches to whom he writes. Leaders are important in any community or organization; good leadership can transform a church and bring fulfilment to God's people. Poor leadership can stifle life and vitality, and kill a community.

Peter gives advice to elders or those with responsibility for a church community. His main concern is that they act in a pastoral way towards their people. They are not to be like military commanders forcing allegiance and imposing discipline; they are to love their congregation and protect and care for them as a shepherd cares for his flock. Peter asks his fellow leaders to be willing and enthusiastic in their care of others. Being dutiful is not enough; people need to know they are loved and cared for. It makes them secure and enables them to grow and flourish spiritually. Bullying tactics are self-defeating. People do not tolerate overbearing demands and hectoring exhortations, even if the demands are correct and the exhortations are justified.

The mode of leadership is important. Pastors or elders should lead like shepherds, with a concern and care for those in their charge, giving guidance and leading wisely.

They are not to use their leadership role to act dishonestly. It is perhaps surprising that so early in the church's existence Peter alludes to the possibility of misuse of position. It seems likely that some cases had already come to light. This is no different from today, when we hear of pastors who have used their position to make themselves wealthy and not always handled finances as transparently as might be helpful.

There is evidence in Peter's day that there were poor leaders who used their role as an opportunity to act superior to those in their charge. For those with a big ego or a fragile personality this is one way to increase self-confidence but it doesn't last long. People quickly see through the façade of superiority, and this will threaten the ego and personality even further.

Christian leaders should be a good example of Christlike living. They should be servant leaders who model godly character and show love and compassion in their leadership. Those who exercise such leadership will be honoured by Christ when he returns. Their service for the kingdom of God is seen and will not go unrewarded.

Peter encourages the younger people to honour those who lead them and be humble, as all should be humble. Those younger people reading this may be a little offended by Peter's comment and rightly say that many young people are as wise as their elders and as obedient to Christ. However, it is a good discipline to respect and listen to the words of those with experience and the benefit of many years of godly living. The lack of respect with which the older generation is treated today is a matter of shame to our communities, and it is a loss since they have much wisdom to pass on. In the church we should value and honour our older people.

Peter sums up all he has been saying by suggesting that leaders and young people should humble themselves. No-one should think too much of themselves; it is God's generosity and kindness that makes us what we are in terms of gifts or abilities. It is God who will raise us up and make us children of the King of Kings, and therefore not something we should seek to do for ourselves.

Finally, in this passage Peter briefly touches on the issue of worry. He reminds his readers to give all their anxieties to God because he cares for them and they do not need to worry – this is so much easier said than done. My pastoral experience suggests to me that Christians worry as much as others; worries about work and family, finances and health, the future and friends, dominate the lives of Christians, and this is not what God wants for us. We should learn the discipline of leaving our anxieties with God, to give God our concerns in prayer each day, and ask him to take them. It may take weeks and months to begin to be released from worry, but it is honouring to God to do this. Worrying about things shows a lack of trust; if we worry, we do not fully believe that God is in control of all that we are and all that we do.

## Questions

1. What are the things that you worry about? How can you help yourself to give your anxieties to God?
2. How far does contemporary church leadership have the qualities and character that Peter advises?
3. Why does strong, confident and even proud leadership seem to enjoy wide support when the biblical pattern for leadership is so different?

# 1 Peter 5:8–14

## Final advice and farewell

---

**Peter concludes his letter with friendly advice, like a parent making sure everything is covered. He warns about the devil and gives a concluding encouragement before he finally signs off.**

---

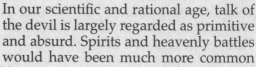
In our scientific and rational age, talk of the devil is largely regarded as primitive and absurd. Spirits and heavenly battles would have been much more common in the culture and language of Peter's world than they are for many today. However, we deny the existence of the devil and ignore his presence at our peril. Bible teaching is clear that there is a spiritual battle, and that the enemy of all that is godly and righteous is the devil, but the devil is subtle and his subterfuge is clever; he can disguise himself as an angel of light and he can be persuasive and beguiling (Genesis 3:1).

Peter therefore warns his readers to be alert and watchful and not to be carried away by excesses of any kind. This will mean always being attentive to the strategies of the devil. Peter depicts the devil as being on the prowl like a lion, seeking vulnerable prey to devour. All people are vulnerable in some way; we all have weaknesses. Our weakness may be pride or self-sufficiency, insecurity or lack of faith, and the devil can work on our weakness to undermine spiritual growth and our trust in God.

The devil can be thwarted by simple obedience to Jesus Christ – by acknowledging the spiritual battles that believers face and recognizing the strategies of the devil when he is attacking. For example, in church leadership meetings, disagreement can easily be manipulated by evil forces so that attitudes and relationships are undermined, and unhelpful comments and opinions are expressed. The devil can fan the flames of misunderstanding to create mistrust and break relationships, but a commitment to love and be patient with one other in discussion can frustrate the devil's plans. When anyone is under pressure, such as the readers of Peter's letter, it gives added scope for stress and tension, and so Peter reminds his readers to stand firm in their faith, accepting that others are also suffering and struggling.

Peter wants to emphasize that his readers are not alone. So often people going through difficulties struggle more, because it seems as if they are alone and that they are the only ones struggling in that way. This is never true. Others struggle and face trials, and are attacked by the devil. Peter encourages his readers to remember that others face the same battles and they are not alone.

Peter puts all the struggles and battles into the context of the greatness of God. The vision of God as great and powerful is never far from Peter's thoughts, and having discussed other things, he always returns to the magnificent God we worship. He speaks of the God of all grace; the God, who even though the devil does attack and seek to trip us up and we do sometimes succumb, is always kind and generous towards us. He is always willing to restore and to sustain us, and even if believers do struggle at times, this amazing God has called us to have a place in eternity. The struggles will pass, they are not for ever. What is for ever is the place in eternity reserved for all who have faith in Christ. This reservation may not be fully available until they have gone through some tough times, but they have the promise that they will be restored and made strong to take their place in the kingdom of God. God has the power to do this; he is gracious and kind, so he will accomplish it for that is what he desires.

As Peter concludes, he makes noteworthy points (verses 12–14). He explains that he has written to encourage his readers, to bear witness that the gospel message is truth from God and to urge them to live faithfully by this truth

– not a bad aim for any pastor. So often we only concentrate on exhorting people to live faithfully, and we forget to encourage them to bear witness to the truth.

Peter mentions that he is helped in the writing of this letter by Silas, who has been a faithful brother and companion on his missionary journeys and preaching tours. Also with him is Mark, who is so precious that he is like a son, although they are not blood relatives. She who is in Babylon is a code name for the church in Rome. Peter would need to exercise some caution, as the church was subject to harassment and misunderstanding. He would not want to make life more difficult than necessary for his community. The Roman authorities may have interpreted such information as a warning that churches were communicating and mobilizing in ways that were detrimental to the Empire.

Peter suggests they greet each other with a holy kiss, or greet each other appropriately for people in a family or close relationship. Such practices are culturally determined, and for many the thought of a holy kiss would be anathema. However, we should find ways to greet each other genuinely as brothers and sisters in Christ. This might be a warm and sincere handshake, a hug or a kiss, but our body language ought to indicate we are more than just acquaintances.

Peter wishes peace to all who are in Christ. Peace is a rich word with broad meaning and resonance. It would include peace with God by having our sins forgiven and being reconciled as his children. It would also refer to peace with others, as love heals relationships. It would involve all the blessings of God's life and presence that the word 'shalom' encapsulates. Peter wishes his readers all the best that God has to offer, a rich blessing indeed.

## Questions

1. At what point in your life are you most vulnerable to attack from the devil? How can you resist such an attack?

2. How can Peter's great vision of God and his incredible greatness be reinforced in our church communities each week?
3. The letter ends on a note of peace – is peace possible in this world unless people understand the grace of God expressed in Jesus Christ?

## Stop and look: Coping with suffering

The issue of suffering is probably the most voiced objection to Christian faith in the Western world. When any event occurs and tragedy befalls innocent communities, commentators raise the question of how anyone can believe in a God of love in the light of such pain and suffering. This happened following the Tsunami in 2004, and when the Chechen rebels laid siege to the school in Beslan and hundreds of children died. Where was God when the innocent were dying and when thousands were traumatized? The rational mind thinks if God is all-powerful he could stop suffering, and if God is all-loving he would stop suffering. Since suffering continues, God cannot exist or cannot be loving. However, this presentation of the problem of suffering is like saying $2 + 2 = 3$. Just because God is loving and powerful does not mean he stops suffering. Peter refers to various instances of suffering, and makes a powerful case for suffering not always being a bad thing.

Pain is necessary to show that there is something wrong. If there were no pain, then a person would not know if he had broken his leg, or someone would not know if she was close to a fire. Pain can be a good indicator both physically and emotionally that something needs dealing with. If there were no pain, I would not feel distress at injustice around the world and would not be moved to do anything about it. The pain of others brings out my compassion and love; if no-one suffered I would never know what compassion is or need to show care and concern.

In Peter's letter he shows that suffering can bring about good things. The prime example is the death and resurrection of Christ. His suffering led to victory over death and the possibility of the forgiveness of sins. Suffering cannot be all bad if through it the world is saved.

In 1:6 Peter speaks of trials, suggesting that minor suffering may be a good thing because it refines our faith and strengthens our character. God is not concerned that this life is comfortable for us; he loves us too much for that. Just as a parent I am concerned that my son grows up to be a godly and mature young man, so God is concerned that each of his children grows to be mature and holy. As a parent I don't always make life easy for my son; I seek to teach him lessons in life that are sometimes hard, and he suffers a little so that he will learn self-discipline, honesty and integrity as well as perseverance and endurance. Similarly God teaches us lessons in life, and at times it feels as if he is making us suffer, but he is seeking to develop a Christlike character within us. This can be a painful process when so much of our character is arrogant and selfish. God gently peels away the layers of self-sufficiency and rebellion through tough circumstances, which we might see as suffering, in order to prepare us for eternal life with him.

The most precious gift we have is our faith in God. Any circumstances that make that faith more pure are to be welcomed and valued, hard as they may be. Peter makes the claim that those who suffer in the body are 'done with sin' (4:1). This is hard to grasp for those of us in a comfort focused culture. In a world which increasingly seeks after every physical luxury, the idea of needing to suffer in the body is a sobering thought. It seems to suggest that the more we gratify our inclination for comfort and ease, the less likely we are to avoid sin. On the other hand, as we struggle with suffering in the body, so we begin to need less physical gratification that might lead to sin. Peter makes an important point – when we suffer we are less likely to be concerned with selfish things, with self-interest, and we are more inclined to God and his purposes. If we have suffered physically, then we may not worry about the little trials of life and think nothing of it if God calls on us to cope in less comfortable conditions. We can focus more clearly on God and his kingdom rather than on ourselves and our comfort. For those who suffer because they are Christians there is a particular reward. God will bless those who suffer with strength and keep them safe (5:10).

As Christians we can understand the benefits of our own suffering, but it is still difficult to understand God's purposes in the seemingly random nature of suffering in our world. The world is fallen, and this has affected creation and means that natural disasters do impact innocent people, but even the suffering of the Tsunami could have been reduced if the world's wealth were shared more equally, and early warning systems had been more widely available in the region. God gets the blame for a considerable amount of suffering that is caused by human error or inequalities.

Suffering can be God's 'megaphone to a dying world' (C. S. Lewis). People won't listen to comments about their need of God when life is going well; sometimes people in pain are more willing to listen. Maybe suffering is a wake-up call to the population of the world of their need to return to their Maker.

In my experience, however well we might have thought through the issue of pain, each new circumstance requires fresh understanding and wisdom to begin to make sense of the situation. Inevitably for people of faith, suffering brings a feeling of helplessness, loss or vulnerability, and Peter's instruction to give our worries to God, to pray and to know his presence is crucial. Suffering will never be an easy topic to handle because it is painful and it hurts, but even from hurt good can come, and God works more powerfully in pain than in health.

# BEWARE OF THE CONMEN

## 2 Peter

# 2 Peter 1:1–11

## Make every effort

---

**It is worth the effort to do all we can to have godly character, for our Saviour is Jesus Christ.**

---

Peter writes to Christians who are surviving but not thriving; they are facing difficulties and pressures from within the church and from without. He
writes as a slave of the gospel and an apostle, and as someone who from his experiences in prison knows the precious value of the faith he has received.

As a follower of Jesus Christ, he acknowledges that like a slave, he has no rights; no sick days, no holidays, no rest days. Peter knows what it is to be beaten and imprisoned, but he knows too the benefits of being enslaved to the perfect slave owner. Peter has given up all rights, in return for the amazing privilege of serving the King of Kings and Lord of Lords.

### Peter – a worried apostle

If Peter is a slave of Christ, he is also a worried apostle (an apostle is someone who walked with Jesus and was set apart to found the church). Peter is concerned that there are fake teachers in the church who are deceiving God's people, offering a bogus gospel that appears attractive, but is damaging and destructive.

False teachers were saying there is an easier way of being a Christian; you don't have to be good all the time. God will forgive you whatever you do. Jesus isn't coming back to judge and punish you if you get it wrong, so do what you enjoy and forget all that the apostles taught. Just like health programmes that appear attractive and easy but do little good, so the false teachers were suggesting things that sounded good but did not deliver. They did not bring the peace and grace that only the true gospel delivers.

## Peter – a clear teacher

Peter is a willing slave and a worried apostle and he is also a clear teacher. In the opening words of the letter, he presents the essence of the gospel (verse 1b) – its source, its core, its worth and its outcome.

**Source**  The source of the gospel is the righteousness of God; his fairness and generous mercy; his gracious kindness and love. That is the starting point – that God loves his people and he is a holy God. The gospel is not made up by human minds; it is the very wisdom of God himself.

**Core**  Jesus Christ, the Messiah is the core of the gospel. Not a radical thought to us if we are used to the idea, but to many at the time this was shocking and amazing. Jesus – not just of Nazareth – but God himself come to save his people.

**Value**  This gospel's value is precious and treasured. Whether a Christian walked with Jesus as the apostles did or had the message handed down as the second-generation Christians did, or whether someone believes 2000 years later, still faith is precious, it is priceless. When people understand what faith means and costs, they recognize its value.

**Outcome**  The outcome is seen in the second title used of Jesus, not just the Christ but also Saviour. Believers are saved from sin, saved to live for

God, and this salvation is gained through the cross.

## Peter – an encouraging pastor

As an apostle, Peter could be assertive, firm, challenging and provocative; as a pastor, he could be affirming, concerned and encouraging. Peter knows that there are issues to face, but first he wants to build his readers up and he speaks of grace and peace.

**Grace** is the generous heart of God who treats people according to his great love, not as they deserve. Peter wants his readers to know the generosity of God in their lives. He wants them to be blessed with all that God gives in abundance.

**Peace:** Peter also wishes them peace in abundance. Authentic faith brings peace with God. It brings a clear change in how Christians see themselves and God. To be at peace with God is to be accepted and loved.

## Knowledge of God

In some ways the opening to this letter is like many others, as it refers to the sender and the recipients, and yet in other ways it is unique. One of the unique features is Peter's reference to the 'knowledge' of God. This is not just knowledge *about* God; this is to know God, to be in a personal relationship with him. This is not to do with being clever or understanding things, it is to do with that knowledge that comes from a heart and life that has been converted to God.

Many believers at the time of Peter liked the idea of Jesus as Saviour, but somehow accepting him as Lord was more difficult. They wanted to know Jesus as Saviour, but then behave immorally and still keep their peace with God. They wanted to live unholy and immoral lives and still receive God's grace. Behind Peter's words is the warning that this is not possible. If they fully know Jesus as Saviour then he is also Lord, and they know they are slaves of the King, who wants not just their belief but their lives lived in harmony with his.

## Power, promises and hard work (verses 3–11)

Peter sees his fellow believers struggling, even though they have knowledge of salvation and God's presence. They need not struggle so much, since those who follow Christ have the power of God available to them, as well as knowledge of God. Through their relationship with God, they can tap into all the resources of heaven, and so with so much to be thankful for, Peter urges his readers to make every effort to receive what is available. It is so common today for people to say 'I need to chill out; I need time for myself.' Peter would suggest that if you want to be fulfilled and contented, then work hard; if you want to know God in your life, make an effort. Peter then lists a whole series of virtues, which we should make an effort to develop, as they are the basis for thriving in a relationship with God:

**Faith and goodness:** the foundation of a Christian's life should be trust in God for everything: money, family, the future and all else, and while trusting God he or she should seek to be a good person, patient and understanding, generous and thoughtful, whatever the circumstances – in the supermarket or behind the steering wheel.

**Knowledge and self-control:** Peter speaks of knowing God (verse 2), using the word *'epignosis'* – having a deep relationship with God. Here he uses the more general word for knowledge, *'gnosis'*. He encourages Christians to know what they believe and to let that knowledge draw them deeper into faith. And that knowledge of God should be accompanied by self-control, in thoughts, language and actions.

**Perseverance and godliness:** how quickly people give up!

Peter encourages his readers to accept difficulties and not lose heart, but to continue despite setbacks and troubles – to persevere and to work towards 'godlikeness'. Authentic faith is characterized by being like Jesus and living differently from others.

**Mutual affection and love:** To all the virtues listed so far, Peter adds brotherly love and compassion for all. Christians are to strive to get on well with others and to honour others by living in a self-sacrificing way. This is a complete contrast to the false teachers, who caused divisions and encouraged self-centredness.

Peter points out that as they grow in character there will be a number of positive consequences. They will be productive in their spiritual lives and not be blinded to the value of authentic faith. Nor will they forget the importance of forgiveness and the truth about the need for salvation.

Although they will make mistakes and get things wrong, God will protect them from falling away. Having been faithful slaves of their Lord, they will receive a rich welcome in the kingdom of God, and like the lost son returning home they will be clothed in fine clothes and have a banquet held in their honour.

## Questions

1. How do the qualities in verses 5–7 impact the way we react to ourselves, to circumstances, to God, to Christians and to others?
2. What does it mean for the church to be effective and productive for the Lord (verse 8)? What might an effective and productive church look like?
3. Peter was concerned for the Christians who were falling away from their faith because of false teachers. Can you think of examples of how people have become short-sighted, blind or forgetful as they lose their spiritual focus (verse 9)?

# 2 Peter 1:12–21

## Be sure: evidence from the apostles and the prophets

---

**The message we hold on to comes from God himself; it is not human in origin.**

---

According to many, we live in an age of spirituality not religiosity. Often people don't want the formalities of church communities or regular worship, which are seen as too human, but they have big questions to ask about God and truth. They want to know why people suffer and about the meaning of life; about the existence of God and how the universe started and how it will end, and also about what happens when someone dies. These are not just twenty-first-century questions, they are timeless questions and Peter touches on at least one or two of them in this passage.

As he writes, Peter knows he is near to death (verses 13–14), but he is not overly worried about this. He is imprisoned in Rome, and the increasing persecution of those who follow Christ and preach the gospel makes his martyrdom inevitable. The *Acts of Peter*, an apocryphal work, records the story of Peter's death by crucifixion with his head down. This is not a readily verifiable tradition, but it is likely that Peter's life did end not long after writing this letter as a result of the Emperor Nero's persecution of the church. As he faces death, Peter has hope in his Lord and Saviour and regards his physical body as a temporary residence, which will be unnecessary when a more permanent place in eternity is ready. However, Peter is concerned for the spiritual well-being of the Christians amongst whom he has worked and to whom he writes. He is concerned that they will remember the essential truth of the gospel message – God's truth.

He emphasizes that their hope in the second coming and the teaching about judgment are not things made up by cunning human minds to control and deceive. He wants them to know that these ideas are the plan and wisdom of God, and he appeals to two sets of evidence to persuade his readers.

The evidence that Jesus is God, the Messiah, and that he will come again, comes from Jesus' own teaching and it is reinforced by the occasion of the Transfiguration witnessed by Peter (verses 17–18). On Mount Tabor Jesus' face and clothes shone with amazing light and brilliance, as if his glory as the Son of God escaped through his humble taking on of human flesh (Mark 9:2–13). On that occasion God affirmed him with the words, 'This is my Son, whom I love; with him I am well pleased', confirming his role as Saviour and triumphant Lord. Peter reminds his readers that he was present at the Transfiguration. He heard what was said and saw what happened. He has not made it up. Their faith is based on eyewitness evidence of what God has said and done.

If the evidence of the apostles is not enough, then Peter urges them to look to the Old Testament prophets as well. In the dark days of Old Testament times, the words of hope that the prophets brought of the Messiah coming were like a bright beam into dark places. The prophets predicted that Jesus would come, and, having come once, that he would come again. Like Venus, the morning star, which catches the first rays of the sun and shows that dawn is on its way, Jesus has come and shown that the dawn of a new heaven and a new earth are on their way. Peter knows a new age is dawning, that God's purposes are being fulfilled, and that believers need to continue in the faith they have received from the apostles and the prophets.

## Answers to big questions

Many people today would say that to believe in God and

to think that Jesus is coming back again, is naïve, just as people said in the first century. Peter argues that what he saw, the teaching he received and the words of the prophets must not be dismissed. It is essential to remember that:

▶ Jesus is Lord, Saviour and Christ.

▶ He is coming back.

▶ He will hold everyone accountable.

## Questions

1. Imagine, like Peter, that you are to be martyred for your faith in a month's time. What would you write to the church back home? Would it be encouragement, warning, teaching or inspiration?
2. Errors had slipped into the church and they were denying the second coming of Christ and disbelieving the judgment of Christ. Are these two errors similarly found in Christian communities today?
3. Read verses 20–21 again carefully – what do they suggest about how Scripture is written? What gives the Bible its authority, and what should govern its interpretation?

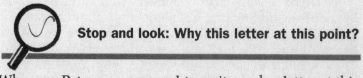

### Stop and look: Why this letter at this point?

Why was Peter so concerned to write such a letter at this time? What is going on to make him put quill to parchment and write these particular thoughts?

It is most likely that this letter was written around thirty years after the death and resurrection of Christ, as Peter approached his own death, thought to have been in AD 66. There are those who think that the letter was written by someone claiming to be Peter, maybe a close follower seeking to continue his teaching and influence, and in that case some would put the date as late as AD 80.

It is thought that these are the words of Peter as he faces imminent death, as the Emperor Nero builds up his persecution of Christians. He is based in Rome but trying to keep in touch with those believers for whom he has apostolic responsibility and amongst whom he worked. Peter writes at this time because he has a particular concern for the purity and orthodoxy of the church community.

Peter is concerned because there are many fake teachers who are deceiving congregations and offering a gospel that has an appearance of attractiveness, but does not offer the life offered by the authentic gospel. This letter is a warning and a reminder. It is set against the background of the early days of Gnosticism, a first-century movement that taught salvation could be gained by acquiring elite knowledge that releases people from the evils of the material world. False teachers were presenting an 'easier' way to be a Christian – a compromised gospel that allowed believers to indulge their greed and sexual immorality and promised God's forgiveness. They also taught that Jesus wasn't coming back to judge and punish, so there was nothing to fear. They emphasized freedom to follow what is enjoyable and forget the apostles' teaching. They did not bring the peace and grace that only the true gospel delivers, and the knowledge they offered was deluded.

As we have seen, many believers were attracted to the idea of Jesus as Saviour, but somehow submitting to him as Lord was less appealing. They wanted to be free to behave immorally and still keep their peace with God. They wanted to live unholy and corrupt lives and still receive God's grace. Peter tells them that this is impossible. They are slaves of the King, who wants them to trust in him and live their lives in harmony with his, to know his peace and grace flowing abundantly into their lives.

**Knowledge of God**

Six times in his second letter Peter refers to 'knowledge' of God or the Lord Jesus Christ. This is a significant emphasis compared to other New Testament writings. Since 2 Peter is a short letter, it is interesting to reflect on the author's focus on knowledge and to think a little about why he emphasizes it so much.

Peter uses two different words for knowledge: '*epignosis*' (1:2; 1:3; 1:8) and '*gnosis*' (1:5; 1:6 and 3:18). There has been much debate about the difference between these two words, and the general consensus is that *epignosis* emphasizes the knowledge that comes from a close relationship with and conversion to God. *Gnosis* focuses more on understanding God and his work in Christ, and his purposes and plans. They go together of course. When believers understand the meaning of who Jesus is, what he taught and how he lived (*gnosis*), then the response should lead to a knowledge of God working in their lives (*epignosis*).

In early Christianity, *epignosis* referred to the understanding or knowledge gained through becoming a servant of Christ. It carried the meaning of a changed perception of God and his purposes and plans through Jesus Christ, alongside a personal knowledge that comes through an ongoing relationship with him.

Peter uses the term *gnosis* to mean the understanding and information that is acquired as a Christian lives faithfully, which increases as the believer matures and learns more. This knowledge feeds the *epignosis* relationship and has ethical and behavioural consequences. One of the reasons that Peter places so much emphasis on knowledge is that knowledge of Christ should lead to holy living, but for the church addressed in this letter, those who claimed to have knowledge, the false teachers, have renounced that knowledge, which is demonstrated by their unholy, corrupt and self-indulgent lives.

For those who follow the words of Peter so many centuries later, a clear knowledge in terms of both personal response and understanding is essential. It is important to know as much of the truth of the gospel as we can, in order to enjoy a deeper and fuller relationship with God through Christ.

Neither of these uses of the word 'knowledge' is necessarily based on intelligence or education. Even in illiterate communities it is possible to pass on the truth of the gospel orally, and for members of the community to grasp the truth and meditate on it, and so gain knowledge that enriches relationships with Christ. However, if we can add to our knowledge by using our intelligence and educational opportunities, then we should do so. Our relationship with God through Christ will be enriched, and we will be effective and productive in our faith (1:8).

Reading the Bible regularly and thinking about its meaning and how it reveals God's purposes and plans helps us to add knowledge to our faith. In addition, prayerful discussion with God about things that we don't understand or cannot quite fathom is yet another means of adding knowledge. An obedient response to God and a quiet trust that his purposes are being fulfilled will lead to our knowledge of God being enriched and deepened.

# 2 Peter 2:1–10a

## Money, sex, power and judgment

**At a vulnerable time for the church, false prophets were denying Christ and living immorally. Like their predecessors, the Old Testament false prophets whose lifestyles dishonoured God, they too would be punished.**

 The themes of money, sex and power fit well in a James Bond film or the TV series Big Brother, maybe even in Parliament or the world of business, where being important and having a huge ego seem to be fundamental. However, the issues of money, sex and power come to us not from the secular world of the twenty-first century but from the world of the church in the first century. Not from the world of media, marketing and millionaires, but the world of faith, fearing God and fulfilment of divine purposes.

Money, sex and power are perhaps the three most alluring factors at work in our lives and communities today, as they have been down the centuries. You may think you are immune to such matters. I tend to think I am too boring to be impacted by such excitement and glamour, and yet the lure of money, sex and power is potentially there for all of us.

**Money issues:** it is so easy to be tempted to massage the truth in order to gain a little extra money: copy that computer file to save buying it; get away with not paying somewhere (their fault – they didn't ask or didn't add up the bill correctly). And what about our job or career? We look for the one that pays the best, but maybe not what is truly best for us. We think life will be so much better if we have more money, and of course, money is comforting and gives us a soft landing in life, but not if we sacrifice our soul in the process; it is too high a price to pay.

**Sex:** we live in a world where sex confronts us all the time. We cannot ignore the sexually tantalizing clothing that is now regularly worn. We are faced with images day in and day out that encourage behaviour that is promiscuous and proud of it. We are sold sex of any kind, with anyone, in any place, as long as they over sixteen, as fun, our right and our need. Those of us who are more restrained or who have tighter boundaries are seen as killjoys, narrow-minded or bigoted.

**Power:** to be powerful is to have the ability to make things happen how and when you want. So the important captain of industry can determine his or her lifestyle, and influence government and communities. But power is not just played out on the big stage of the public arena. Power plays a role in the intimate relationships of husband and wife, parents and children, siblings, friends, work colleagues and social acquaintances. There are those who are addicted to power and to being in control, and there is a bit of this in all of us – thinking we are right, wanting things how we want them because we know best, of course.

## How does this fit with Peter's letter?

The church Peter wrote to was a community of ordinary people who had responded to the extraordinary God. Then false teachers arrived who disturbed the community that had experienced so much of God's love and peace. Symptoms of their false teaching shown in their attitudes to money, sex and power are the very same issues facing the church today.

The contemporary church struggles with teaching on human sexuality, causing tensions in denominations. With respect to money, some church leaders draw huge salaries and have dubious expenses. There are also the tensions between powerful churches and not-so-powerful communities. For the church in the first century, things were not so different. The first flush of church growth and excitement had passed, and then people needed to persevere and cope with ideas being introduced that compromised faith.

There was the issue of the false teachers not acknowledging the full authority of Jesus as Messiah and Lord, which led to inappropriate sexual behaviour. The early Christians were being told that since Jesus had not come back, he would not be coming back, and he would not judge them, so they could live as they pleased and indulge in sensual activity without fear of offending God. They argued that God had created a world to be enjoyed, that they should live a pleasure-filled life, enjoying all that God had given. They were taught that sex was for enjoyment and they should enjoy their bodies without constraint, and so the false teachers led the way by indulging in shameful acts (verse 2).

The false teachers were also motivated unhelpfully by money and the desire to be powerful. To be a teacher in first-century Greek culture was to have status and to be well paid. In verses 3 and 10 they are described as greedy, bold and arrogant, and consequently they were able to gain power over the vulnerable and weak. The teaching they presented was whatever would make them most wealthy and enable them to persuade and manipulate others. So they had a selective approach to the gospel, avoiding the less comfortable aspects such as being judged or living holy lives. This had a certain appeal although it was empty and powerless. Sadly, money, sex and power were as much at work in the first century as in the twenty-first.

Peter is concerned that the believers will accept this wrong teaching and example, deny Christ and forfeit all the blessings that are theirs as Christians. The church was going through tough times; perseverance was difficult and the new ideas were attractive. Peter warns them that those who lead others astray are condemned; they will be destroyed and will face the consequences of their actions. Previously those who had rebelled or mocked God were punished, showing that God deals with those who disregard what is right. Peter gives three examples:

**Fallen angels** (verse 4): this refers back to Genesis 6:1–4 and to Jewish apocalyptic writing. It is an unclear and hazy part of the early beginnings of community life, but it suggests that angels and other supernatural beings did what was wrong; they lusted after the women they saw and were punished for their wrongdoing.

**In the time of Noah** (Genesis 6:6–11): society was evil, people were selfish and no-one cared at all for others. Unbridled lust, power-seeking and worship of money led to God destroying all he had created apart from Noah and his family.

**Sodom and Gomorrah**: Lot, the nephew of Abraham, was living in the city of Sodom (Genesis 19), where rape and violence were routine, and visitors were abused and ill-treated. God determined to destroy Sodom and Gomorrah for their evil and wickedness, and they have become a byword for corrupt society ever since.

Since God did not spare the angels, nor the people of the world, nor the evil cities. Similarly he will not overlook the evil that occurs in other generations.

The church was facing pressure from the outside, being persecuted by the authorities and menaced by those who opposed them. They also faced fifth columnists, those within the church who undermined their purpose and teaching. It began with the denial of basic doctrines and it led on to immoral and abusive behaviour.

### Questions

1. What five warning signs does Peter identify to help his readers spot false teachers?
2. What is it about false teachers that makes them popular with some and so unpopular with the apostles?
3. God judged and punished rebellious angels, evil people in Noah's time and the corrupt cities of Sodom and Gomorrah. Why do people today struggle with the issue of God's judgment and punishment?

# 2 Peter 2:10b–22

## Bold, arrogant and reckless

**Peter describes the false teachers as irresponsible and destructive. It would have been better if they had never heard of Jesus Christ.**

 Being described as bold, arrogant and reckless has a certain appeal, but for the apostle Peter they are words of condemnation and warning – such warnings are relevant today. The former editor of an international fashion magazine commented recently in a television interview: 'Neither Christianity nor Islam is the biggest religion today, it's fashion.' Ken Livingstone, the Mayor of London, was reported as saying 'Anyone who believes in an afterlife should be banned from politics.' We might find these comments mildly amusing because they are bold and a little reckless; on the other hand, they may be a symptom of something worrying and dangerous.

Peter wrote his letter in the most forceful language,

because he was concerned about deceptive ideas coming from within the church. The false teachers were arrogant and contemptuous of all others, despite their own immorality. They ridiculed powers such as demons and laughed at the thought that the devil could have power to mislead them. The misguided teachers were brazen and unaware of the danger they were in; like those who claim they can take their drink or cope with hard drugs and not face difficulties or addiction, so the false teachers claimed they could behave as they liked and they would never be judged because they were above such things.

## Dry wells and hazy mists

Having denounced these fraudsters as brute beasts of instinct, adulterous seducers and experts in greed, Peter likens them to Balaam who was tempted by the offer of wealth to misguide God's people (Numbers 22).

The false teachers were offering the pretence of freedom, which allowed them to feed their appetite for money, immoral behaviour and power, but the freedom they offered could never be realized. It was an illusion and the path led to a dead end. Once they went down this path, they were enslaved to wrongdoing, to corruption and to the plans of evil powers. True freedom could never be found this way.

Peter describes the false teachers as being like wells, looking as though they offered fresh water and could satisfy a thirst, but in fact they were dry and empty. Or they were like a hazy mist that appeared to offer some comfort from the heat of the day, but it offered nothing; it just blew away and the penetrating heat did its worse.

For Peter, the sad fact is that these people had known the truth about Jesus as Lord and Saviour; they had heard of his return and judgment. But they had chosen to ignore it, so they are in a worse state than before they ever heard the good news of Jesus Christ. They were more culpable than when they were in complete ignorance; the judgment that comes their way will not be comfortable.

### Empty, dry wells today

What is the false teaching that can delude us today? In the previous passage we were reminded of the errors of teaching that promotes money, sex and power, and there is a real danger today of Christians justifying ungodly behaviour in these areas. Many of the wrong ideas come from a self-obsessed society. Western culture focuses on the individual, and we have increasingly become a 'me' society where everyone is encouraged to think only 'about me'. In subtle and damaging ways, this false teaching comes into church communities and damages the foundations of the gospel on which the church is built – Jesus Christ as Saviour and Lord.

Teachers and leaders may package contemporary ideas in a Christian wrapper that turns them into false teaching. They may suggest that God wants *me* to be happy so I should do what makes me comfortable. I should recognize that God cares about me, so I should put myself at the centre. I don't need to feel guilty when I do wrong because God forgives me. I should do what suits me; what feels good to me; what blesses me.

All this has a veneer of spirituality and yet it is horribly wrong. God wants his people to be holy and blessed, and that will lead to happiness, but often happiness comes only by taking the route which is less comfortable – 'small is the gate and narrow the road that leads to life' (Matthew 7:13–14).

God cares about his people but that doesn't mean we can put ourselves at the centre. Putting yourself at the centre is the worst thing you can do. Put God at the centre and everything else will work out in the best way as far as God's plans are concerned (Matthew 6:33). This means don't do what is necessarily the easiest or most comfortable, but do what God wants – that is the best way to live.

When we do wrong God does forgive us, but there should be a sense of guilt for disappointing God and getting things wrong. These things matter; they are not unimportant. The false teaching is arrogant and reckless because it suggests that I should do what suits me, what feels good to me, what blesses me. The problem is that we are often very poor judges of what is good for us. Our feelings are poor indicators of what is right and holy.

The well that offers life-giving water that refreshes the soul and the spirit and gives eternal life is the well that is supplied by Jesus – Saviour, Lord and King. And every gulp of that water that you take will renew and restore.

## Questions

1. Peter describes the false teachers as reckless and arrogant. Reflect on occasions when you have tended towards such attitudes and how it affected your spiritual life.
2. Freedom is a much-abused word these days – freedom of speech, freedom to choose, freedom of conscience and belief – what is the danger of freedom as Peter would see it? What does Christian freedom mean?
3. The false teachers were free to be greedy, to indulge their lust and to exercise power. What makes that kind of freedom both attractive and disappointing?

# 2 Peter 3:1–10

## A salutary reminder

---

**Even if it seems as if God is delayed in his purposes, the readers are reminded to hold on to the truth that Jesus will return and fulfil all God's promises.**

 In all the rush and bustle of life it is easy to forget things: appointments, shopping, birthdays, things that need doing, and maybe more importantly it is easy to forget why anything matters. Peter writes this second letter to his friends to remind them of things they might have forgotten. Like everyone on planet earth, it is so easy to know something, to know it is important, and yet, because of the demands of the immediate or issues that press upon us, it is forgotten and neglected.

Peter reminds his readers to recall the life-changing words of the prophets and the apostles: those words of life and transformation that matter so much and can so easily be overlooked. The problem is that many other messages are broadcast into our lives, and it is difficult to hold on to what is important because so much else clogs our thoughts.

When people are surrounded by those who distort or mock the gospel, it is hard to remember the truth. It is hard to hold on to what is right when people question and challenge what Christians believe. Peter warns that those who ridicule people of faith and their belief that Jesus will return and will judge everyone have themselves forgotten how the world began. They have forgotten that God created the world and the heavens by his Word, and by that same Word the heavens and earth will be judged, and all that is temporary and ungodly will be destroyed. Peter reminds his readers that they are to expect people to jeer at Christian truth. They are to expect those who make fun of godly values and holy living.

Peter then reminds them of God's timing; 'a day is like a thousand years, and a thousand years are like a day' (verse 8). By my estimation that means it could be less than two days since the resurrection. I don't know a single person who isn't impatient for God to act in some way or other. We are impatient for God to show those who ridicule his truth that he is the Sovereign Lord. We are impatient for God to heal or to answer prayer, to bring to faith or to restore vision and expectation. We don't understand why God doesn't work more quickly, and that is largely because our time frame is different to God's. His purposes are being fulfilled. His plans will come to fulfilment at the perfect time, and we need to be reminded that we don't know better than God, that our patience will be rewarded and that all the prophets foretold and the apostles passed on is true.

After much impatient waiting and anxious anticipation, the Day of the Lord will come. The world as we currently know it will end. It will be sudden, it will take most by surprise and it will have cosmic consequences. Jesus spoke of it and the prophets predicted it, and Peter reminds his readers not to forget it. The more we are reminded of the teaching of the gospel, the more we will be stimulated to wholesome thinking (verse 1). The more we remind ourselves of the truth of God's Word, the greater our protection from the destructive influences of the world in which we live. We all need reminders of what matters, and Peter's reminder is particularly relevant in a world where so many voices threaten to drown out the truth of Christian faith.

## Questions

1. Peter wants the believers to be stimulated to wholesome thinking (verse 1). What is wholesome thinking

and what things lead you to unwholesome thinking?
2. Who are those ridiculing or mocking the message of the gospel today? What response should the church make to them?
3. Peter speaks confidently of the 'Day of Judgment' or 'Day of the Lord' (verses 7 and 10). What does he suggest this day will be like? Why do people have difficulty with the concept of such a day?

**The end of the world**

Speaking with conviction or concern about the end of the world usually ensures a wide berth by others. It is too immense a subject to think about, and most people would suggest that it is a scientific matter about which we can and do know very little. To claim some understanding of how the world might end and what the purposes of the ending of the world might be is to put oneself in the same grouping as those who watch for fairies or hunt out UFOs. And yet the second letter of Peter along with other biblical writing is clear and specific that the world will end and that there are signs to look for.

There is a consensus amongst scientists and theologians that the world will end. In some circles, it is thought it will happen in about 10 billion years time, if it hasn't happened before then. The biblical perspective supported by Peter is that the ending of the world will be purposeful, intentional and necessary for God's plans to be fulfilled. Jesus will come back. He will come not as a sacrificial Lamb of God, but as the victorious King, and will introduce a new era, a new heaven and a new earth, with continuity in some way to this earth and universe, and yet totally renewed and recreated. We don't know what the end of the world will be like. We have images and big hints, but it is so far beyond what we can grasp now that it is impossible for us to comprehend fully or make sense of it.

Christian teaching about the return of Christ and a day of judgment was under attack 2000 years ago, and many continue today in a similar vein to criticize and mock those who believe in the second coming of Christ and a time when everyone will be answerable to God. Many people think that Christians are quaint or naïve because they believe in such things.

For those outside the family of faith, it is attractive to disregard any moral or spiritual accountability for how they live. If the idea is dismissed that God would one day ask why people are greedy or proud, selfish or arrogant, full of hatred and unjust, then that poor behaviour doesn't matter.

As far as morality and sin are concerned, things have not changed much in 2000 years. The same issues lead people into disgrace and difficulty. The same issues tempt and distract. Those who say to us in so many words 'you cannot believe such things; God cannot be like that' have a vested interest in the answer. They don't want to believe that God might ask them some tough questions, because they don't have ready answers. If there is no judgment, then many would say it doesn't matter how you live today. Christian teaching insists that it does matter how you live; everyone will answer for their behaviour, this world will end, and a day of accountability will occur.

Peter is clear about the main themes of the Day of the Lord, God's judgment and the concluding events of this earth. The Day of the Lord will be God's final intervention in the affairs of humanity. He will punish sin, restore the faithful and establish his rule over all empires. This day is linked with the return of Christ and will be accompanied by cosmic signs and environmental upheaval.

On that day (1:11), those who are faithful followers of Christ will be welcomed into God's eternal kingdom. They will be judged faithful, and rewarded for their faithfulness. Peter also makes a clear case for God's judgment on those who are not forgiven. Although angels are higher spiritual beings, they were judged and punished for their wrongdoing (2:4). The people in the time of Noah and

Sodom and Gomorrah were punished for their wickedness. Peter indicates that those who speak blasphemously, behave immorally and act rebelliously against God will be judged and punished.

Peter refers to the Day of the Lord (3:10), which is an idea clearly taught from the Old Testament (Joel 3:12–14), affirmed by Jesus (Mark 13:26–27) and then reinforced here by Peter. A day will come when all that is temporary is destroyed, and all people are called before the presence of God. Those who know Christ as Lord and Saviour will enjoy the rewards of eternal life with God. Those who have rejected Christ as Saviour and Lord will not. The Day of the Lord and God's judgment appear delayed so that even more might come to faith and respond to God's offer of eternal life (3:9).

# 2 Peter 3:11–18

## Live well now and live for ever

**Be careful to maintain godly qualities so that you are not carried away by destructive influences.**

 The world as it is currently known will come to an end, and Peter uses cosmic images to portray the ending of the present order and the arrival of the new heaven and new earth with righteousness at its core. With uncompromised confidence, Peter insists that the disciples of Jesus make every effort to be ready by being blameless, at peace with God and full of hope.

It seems that being blameless gets a bad press these days, because it sounds boring and tedious. I wonder why that is? Peter is encouraging people to live holy lives, not just because of fear of judgment, but in order to be prepared and ready for eternity; the new heaven and earth are anything but boring – filled with all the best parts of life, love, beauty, peace and wonder.

Peter is horrified that people in the church have been misled into thinking that since Jesus has not yet come back he is not coming back. The apparent delay in Jesus returning is actually because he wants to give more time for people to come to him. Further, Peter is worried that they have been wrongly taught that there will be no judgment and that it doesn't matter how they live because God will still forgive them.

Peter uses the authority of the apostle Paul to support what he is saying. Paul also wrote that the time before the second coming would be a time for turning to God in repentance and receiving Christ. Peter suggests that the false teachers cannot understand or grasp Paul, because they do not have the basic teaching in the faith; they are untrained and blind guides. For all their pretensions to be teachers, these speakers have not bothered to acquire sufficient knowledge to understand Paul or other Christian teaching. So they misinterpret simple Christian truth and consequently teach error.

## Characteristics of living well

**Holy** (verse 11): To be holy is to be set apart for God and set apart from this world, with a purity and grace that are attractive. Truly holy people are full of love and life, people of joy and celebration as well as purity and Christ-centredness.

**Godly** (verse 11): To be godly is to be like God and includes so many things. It is to be creative, enjoying beauty and wonder. It is to love and build others up and to work towards a better world. It is to live a good and pure life, seeking to honour Christ and please him, and be prepared for the new heaven and new earth.

**Forward-looking** (verse 11): This means never to lose sight of the eternal dimension to this life and to keep in mind the knowledge of Christ's return and that 'the best is yet to come'.

**Be at peace and spotless** (verse 14): To be spotless before God and at peace with him is to be forgiven and to keep a short account with him. It is to avoid behaviour that is wrong and damaging. When believers fail, they can speedily seek forgiveness and restoration of their relationship.

### The final words of Peter

These are not the words from a deathbed scene, but they are the final recorded words of someone who knew he had days, weeks or at most months still to live. Even in that context there is no sentiment or self-indulgence; he remains a consistent servant of God and leader in the church. His concern is not for himself but for the people God has entrusted to his charge. He is passionate for their well-being in Christ; he is committed to caring for them and supporting them to the end. He warns them again to guard against faulty ideas, he encourages them to grow in grace and understanding and he ends with words of worship and honour to Jesus Christ himself.

Ordinary letters tend to wind down at the end, but letters for public reading often summarize the major themes of the letter, and this is what Peter does.

### You have been warned

Many of us are far too complacent about spiritual issues. We may look at others and be grateful that we haven't fallen into the traps which have ensnared them. However, everyone needs to be alert to ideas that are damaging. Just the other day I spoke with someone whose life was in a big mess, and she said 'but I read my Bible notes every day' – as if reading a brief paragraph were all that

Christian obedience and discipleship is about. There are things that trip us spiritually and we should be alert to such things. If we think we are safe and secure, then we are in a vulnerable position.

There will always be people who will chip away at the faith and confidence people have in God: those who seek to shape beliefs and mould lifestyles so they fit more comfortably with this fallen and damaged world rather than with God's perfection, holiness and love. It will start innocently enough: a reasonable sort of idea, a clear argument, but it could end in serious issues of failure. Be alert, says Peter, to those who would drag others away from faith with short-term appealing ideas.

When Peter wrote this letter people outside the community of faith thought it naïve and simplistic to believe that Jesus would come again and that there would be a Day of Judgment. Similarly today, many people think Christians are quaint because they believe Jesus will return and that all will stand before God and answer to him for how they have lived.

For those outside the family of faith, it is attractive to disregard any moral or spiritual accountability as restrictive and oppressive. Those who say 'you cannot believe such things, God cannot be like that,' have a vested interest in the answer. They don't want to believe that God might ask them some tough questions, because they don't have easy answers.

It is easy to be deceived by those who suggest that the Christian lifestyle is prudish or unnatural. The argument that you need to experience things and live life to the full and satisfy appetites can be appealing. Be warned, Peter would say to believers today, because the world can trick people. Even sincere believers can give in to temptation and be attracted by quick-fix ideas about the Christian life that are false and destructive.

### Grow in grace and knowledge

It is impossible to stand still as a Christian; we either grow and deepen our relationship, or we wither. We are either moving closer to God and being shaped and moulded into the likeness of Christ, or we are following the patterns of this world and becoming like the world that has rejected godliness and truth. We have to work on this growth, for we have an inbuilt tendency to push Jesus into the background of our lives as other things crowd in. We have to make a deliberate and constant effort to bring him to the front of our being, so his presence determines our thinking and shapes our understanding, responses and attitudes.

A man facing death takes care to say what matters. His words are worth noting, and in following them, you will bring glory and honour to God.

### Stop and look: Bogus teaching

Teaching and ideas come to us from a seemingly infinite number of sources. Even within the Christian community, the channels of communication are endless: conferences and services, God channels on TV, CDs, DVDs, books, magazines and radio. How much of what we hear is bogus or false teaching? How do we discern what is right and what is wrong, when even within the church opinion is divided?

The novel *The Da Vinci Code* took the world by storm because it was a good story, but it is totally fictitious. The gullible were drawn into the plot, and in the excitement of the drama believed some of the bizarre ideas it portrayed, so much so that when it was made into a film, it was banned in a number of places. A little thought and investigation would indicate that the substance of Dan Brown's story was created simply to entertain. The fact that he used genuine place names and historical buildings is confusing, but it does not take much research to discover that the plot and the themes have no historical basis or supporting evidence.

However, other bogus teaching is a little more complicated. The moral issues of sexuality and family values are dividing the church in numerous places, and the continued questioning of the role of Christ, and in particular his divinity, is teaching that has gained significant hold in a number of university departments. The teaching that Christians should not suffer is also a cause for concern; it holds that Christians should prosper materially and expect the best, and that physical healing is for everyone who believes and has faith.

One of the issues that worried Peter was that the bogus teachers claimed there would be no judgment, and if there is no judgment then it doesn't matter how people live. Similarly today, the idea of judgment is viewed as medieval, and most contemporary minds would think it belonged to a different era. Current thinking has little room for punishment or retribution; the focus is on forgiveness, restitution and finding reasons why people behave unhelpfully, but not blaming them.

The absence of belief in judgment may appear minor in itself, but it may lead to more serious consequences. If there is no judgment, then behaviour is without boundaries and curbs. It is then easy to be deceived by those who suggest that the Christian lifestyle is too restrictive, prudish or even unnatural. The argument that you need to live life to the full and satisfy your appetites is persuasive.

False teaching arose because of teachers who were arrogant, greedy and immoral. They twisted the truth in order to line their pockets, to gain control over others and to indulge their appetites for both food and sex without restraint. It would appear that much of the false teaching today has similar motivation: the desire to gain wealth and power, or to indulge appetites inappropriately. Their doctrines and ideas may be wrapped up in persuasive words and clever images, but if they do not concur with the teaching of the Bible, then they are bogus and will be damaging in the long run.

There is a danger in our warm, embracing and inclusive communities that we are not alert to the influence of false teaching. The issue is even more relevant today as teachers of all kinds travel around the world making impressive claims and communicating interesting ideas. Followers of Christ need to be wise and careful as they listen, and ensure that what they are taught is the truth.

## Stop and think: Holy living

The false teachers that dominate Peter's thoughts as he writes his letter reveal their error, in part, by their unholy living. Peter condemns them as greedy, indulging in evil pleasures in broad daylight, revelling in deceitfulness and full of lust. These people are the examples that many Christian disciples were tempted to follow. It is a disturbing matter. Peter does not develop the theme of holy living in great detail, but it is implicit in his writing, and it is an important reminder for believers today when so many of the influences facing us are identical to the behaviour of the false teachers of Peter's day.

In some church circles, there is a tendency to encourage a compromised discipleship that is soft on sin and emphasizes grace and forgiveness. While grace and forgiveness are always at the heart of God and he is merciful and generous in all things, he is also holy and offended by sin. Peter makes the point (3:11), declaring that since all that surrounds Christians in the world is going to pass away and one day God's purposes will be perfectly fulfilled, believers should live holy lives now in order to be prepared for the new heaven and the new earth. Peter encourages his congregation to make every effort to live a pure and blameless life while they wait for God to complete his purposes. He tells them to be decent and to be at peace with God – in other words, live holy lives in order that they might please God and live well.

Many seem to regard holy living as restrictive and limiting. A false understanding of living a holy life can make it appear that all the excitement and pleasures of life are denied, and all that is tedious and constrained is permitted. How far from the truth of a holy life! True holiness is to live as God first intended, in love, peace, truth and depth of understanding. It is to be conscious of the power and creativity of God alongside his eternal plans and purposes. It is to be a person of wisdom and grace, enjoying all the insights and experiences of life in a constructive and wholesome way. It is to live life to the full; exciting, adventurous, stimulating and satisfying; to know God and walk with him in faith and trust, not behaving in a way that is hurtful or damaging to oneself or others.

If we want to be fit to live with God for eternity, then we ought to begin to prepare now. We ought to make every effort with those weaknesses that offend God and those attitudes that displease him. The Holy Spirit works in us if we will co-operate and let our inner being be transformed, so that our thoughts and actions are increasingly the thoughts and actions of God himself.

Holiness is not an added extra for Christian discipleship or an advanced module for those who have reached a certain level of maturity. It is the best way to live for all of God's people, and it is the standard to which all believers should aspire.

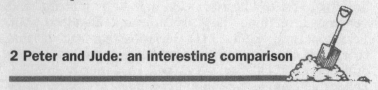

## 2 Peter and Jude: an interesting comparison

It is interesting to compare 2 Peter and Jude; of the twenty-five verses that make up the letter of Jude, fifteen similar verses appear in Peter's second letter. You notice as you read through that there are similar themes, illustrations and comments, and yet there are also significant differences.

Both letters were written in the latter part of the first century, at a time of social upheaval and turmoil when churches were vulnerable to false ideas and wrong thinking. As the circumstances developed which led to the fall of Jerusalem in AD 70, the local church which had been centred on Jerusalem was dispersed and the fledgling community of believers was scattered. Some blind guides took the opportunity to infiltrate churches as a soft target to make a living and behave dubiously.

Theologians have compared the two letters in great depth and here are some helpful conclusions:

▶ Jude was probably written first, using sources that were well known at the time.

▶ While they both had access to the same sources and Peter may even have had Jude's letter before him, they did have slightly different ideas in mind in their writing and thinking.

▶ Despite their similarities, they are both unique letters written for different settings.

They have the following themes in common:

1. Condemnation of phoney leaders or false teachers who were making a living by teaching wrong ideas about the gospel, denying the lordship of Christ and behaving in a flagrantly sinful manner and proud of it. In both 2 Peter and Jude, those who teach wrong ideas as God's truth are likened to Old Testament false prophets and will incur the same judgment (2 Peter 2:1–9). Jude 4 reflects the same concern about those who 'pervert God's grace' through false teaching and godless lifestyles. Both Jude 18 and 2 Peter 3:3–4 refer to those who mock the gospel and scoff at ideas such as Jesus returning.

2. The denial of the authority of the apostles by false teachers and their appealing argument offering freedom

and experience not previously known. Jude 17 refers to the words and authority of the apostles as those who defined the faith and possessed great understanding.

3. An agreed content to apostolic faith which has an authority above other teaching and ideas, towards which the false teachers are antagonistic or even mocking. Jude 3 speaks of 'contending for the faith', the implication being that there is an agreed content to the beliefs and gospel that followers of Christ adhere to. Later in verse 18, Jude recognizes there are those who mock such agreement and understanding.

4. An insistence on the need to make an effort as a disciple of Christ. Peter in his second letter (1:5 and 3:14) stresses that individual believers should do all they can to co-operate in the process of discipleship and being made godly. This is not something that comes about passively, without endeavour; it has to be worked at. Jude (3 and 20–23) encourages his readers actively to participate in maintaining the faith and remaining in God's love; they are to make an effort to fulfil all their potential as children of God.

5. Both Jude and 2 Peter express a horror about the consequences of a false understanding of faith, which will lead to condemnation and judgment. Jude 7 and 15 refer to those who face punishment because of their failure to obey God, and the terminology is graphic and horrific to show the danger of disobedience and rebellion before God. 2 Peter 2:4 and 3:10 focus on the dangers of facing judgment for disobeying God and misleading others.

## Themes specific to Jude

▶ There is a particular emphasis about communities being undermined by false teaching and false hope, and being corrupted from within by bogus leadership.

▶ Jude is concerned to teach how communities can be built up and protected from compromised faith and teaching.

## Themes specific to 2 Peter

▶ Peter shows a particular concern for individual followers of Christ and their standing before God in the light of damaging teaching.

▶ He emphasizes that godly people can be protected and kept by God in the midst of struggles and difficulties.

▶ Peter focuses on true knowledge of Christ and his purposes, and the importance of the Day of the Lord.

# FIGHT FOR THE FAITH

*Jude*

# Jude 1–2

## A golden hello!

---

**Jude opens his letter with simple words of truth, which have the potential to inspire even when faith is tested most rigorously.**

---

Have you ever gone through a rough patch in church life? Then maybe the opening words of this letter can help you. Jude writes to believers facing diffi  culties, and as they struggle with issues, the letter comes to soothe and encourage. It is the kind of greeting that brings a smile to the face and warmth to the soul.

It is a reminder that their faith is an anchor that will hold them, and in the turmoil of their present situation, they are encouraged to stand back and see the big picture of God using them.

**They are loved by God**. Despite the pain of division and controversy within the Christian community, this is the present reality; they are literally 'in God's love'– a complicated little phrase which means 'loved by' and 'loved in God'. In an insecure world where no-one quite knows what this afternoon might bring, let alone tomorrow, they have the security of knowing that they are loved and embraced by the Lord God.

This idea of being loved would have had a very familiar ring to it. Israel, the great people of God in the Old Testament, were called and loved every step of the way. The church of the New Testament had a great heritage, and they could look back and see how God had worked out his purposes over many generations.

As we look back, we see that we don't stand alone as a

generation of God's people. We stand in the great promises of God over the centuries, over the millennia, and we see how our spiritual connections go back maybe 6,000 years or more. The truth is that we are loved in the present, but we see God's hand of love in every generation; it reaches back into the furthest history.

**Kept for Jesus Christ.** Those to whom Jude writes are not only loved but kept secure for the future when Jesus comes again – not secure in the sense of wealth, fame or success; but even if they are poor, despised failures, God has not let go and will not let go.

Jude was worried about the church. He saw it being flooded with all kinds of false ideas and wrong teaching, and yet he encouraged his people, knowing that God would keep a firm hold on those who responded to him.

Despite all the difficulties of trying to remain faithful and obedient in a faithless and disobedient age, God has the power to bring all who believe through to eternity. There is no need to follow the lemming-like behaviour of others. God will hold firm to his people and bring them into his presence, spotless and without blemish.

**They are called** to be part of the family of God. God's community is loved and kept in a real sense, so that they might fulfil their calling to be the people of God. This is not a casual or informal matter – it is to be set apart, identified and wanted by God. All who have come to know Jesus Christ as Saviour and Lord have been summoned by God, and he has requested their presence in his family. You might receive an invitation to a wedding, and that is exciting and makes you feel wanted, but this calling has a much greater meaning than an invitation. It is an irresistible request to join God in his kingdom; it is a call to be part of God's incredible purposes, to be loved and kept as their Maker intended them to be.

Jude encourages the little gathering of believers, reminding them that though they may not feel very special, and while they may not seem very strong and there may be difficulties and troubles all around, yet they are special. The sovereign Lord of the universe has called them to be a part of his family.

Jude concludes his opening greetings with a prayer for the people to whom he writes. He wants them to know the merciful presence of God, who does not treat anyone as they deserve, but is forgiving and generous. He prays for the people of God to know his mercy, particularly in the tough times they face.

He asks that they might know peace – that harmony of body and soul with God and his purposes which is preferable to anything else. We live in a world where there is so little peace, so little inner security, so little harmony with our Maker – it is a prayer for today as much as it was for the first century.

The third prayer request is for love. Love is a common word, cheapened by overuse and abuse in today's society. In Jude's letter love is used with a particular focus in mind. As the emphasis of the letter is keeping and preserving those with faith, so God's love is focused on bringing us into his presence safe and sound, and keeping us there. It is like the radar on an aircraft which keeps the plane on the right flight path and brings it safely into land on the right runway. This is not an indulgent, anything goes sort of love, but a holy, tough love that desires the best for everyone and wants as many as possible to know peace and fulfilment.

Jude opens his letter in a golden way – the warmth of God's presence shines through. He knows life isn't easy for those who read the letter, but they are secure, having been called, loved and kept. He prays that they might also receive huge measures of God's generous care, his reconciling power and his deep fulfilling love. Those words are also for us each day, as we walk as God's people.

1. What does it mean for you to be loved and kept, that you might fulfil your calling?
2. How can church communities use Jude's opening words to aid worship and prayer?
3. There is a modesty in the way Jude describes himself, a servant of Jesus Christ and a brother of James. He doesn't mention his leadership role or that he is a half-brother of Jesus. What can we learn from his example about humility in high places, and does he offer an antidote to the cult of celebrity that seems to pervade our culture?

# Jude 3–7

## Love talks tough

**A warning about false teachers and the need to fight for the truth of the faith.**

 In some circles, Christians are regarded as the relations everyone loves, because they never say anything that isn't warm, agreeable and pleasant. It therefore comes as a bit of a shock when Jude writes things that people don't want to hear and don't like, but are necessary. Jude exposes corrupt and evil people for what they are. The pleasantries are over and Jude focuses on those with destructive ideas and doubtful morality. He wanted to write about faith in positive terms, but the urgent need was to write about protecting the faith.

Teachers who saw themselves as the elite have infiltrated the little church community to whom Jude writes.

They consider themselves to be more mature and sophisticated than others, and above the rules and boundaries that others kept to – so much so that they thought they could be immoral and greedy, believing that such things didn't impact their spiritual life. They were conmen, deceiving themselves and others.

They taught that the gospel message is about total freedom today with the expectation of total forgiveness tomorrow. Their bad theology and bad thinking led them to bad morals and behaviour – the kind of behaviour that would shock you if you read about it in the tabloid press, let alone discovered it in the church.

Christian freedom is freedom *from* sin and freedom to know the rule of Christ; not freedom *to* sin. The root of the problem for the wandering teachers was that they refused to bow the knee to Christ and acknowledge him as Lord; they were wilfully rebellious. They did what was easiest for them, not what was right or best.

Similar thinking is found today when people like the singer Mary J. Blige are heard to say, 'My God is a God who wants me to have things. He wants me to bling. He wants me to be the hottest thing on the block. I don't know what kind of God the rest of y'all are serving' (*The Times*, 19 April 2006).

## Confusion flourishes

We might think it couldn't happen today – and it wouldn't happen in the same way. We don't have the same sort of teachers wandering from place to place, selling their ideas and being supported by those who listen. However, there are constant messages coming to us through the media – some excellent, some not. And we all pay for ideas one way or another. There are lifestyle coaches and the latest self-help books, which often have a spiritual veneer and are appealing and attractive, but they are not a good basis for faith and biblical understanding.

There are times when we need to fight to defend our faith; when we need to protect the truth of the gospel against those who would seek to undermine and defeat it. We need to be aware that those who deceive others and rebel themselves are answerable to God, and will have to account for their behaviour to him, but we must play our part too.

### Defend the faith

Jude says 'contend for the faith that was once for all entrusted to the saints' (verse 3). What is it we are to defend? Faith in Jesus? Belief that Jesus is the Son of God? Acceptance of heaven and hell, judgment, punishment, eternal damnation? Where do we draw the line about what we should defend and what we should leave as a grey area that we are unsure about? There seem to be so many grey areas. Which battles should we fight and which should we leave?

I think my litmus test would be that I would work alongside people who confess Jesus Christ as Saviour and Lord, and who seek to live according to his teaching. This leaves many questions unanswered and many loose ends. So I draw my line in what I think is a fairly inclusive place. But as one writer put it, 'wherever you draw the line you will always find Jesus on the other side'.

The trouble for Jude was that even in drawing the line in such a way as to include all those who simply had faith in Jesus as Saviour and Lord, there was a whole raft of people who could not be included, and some who were in the church and shouldn't have been allowed to be in positions of authority.

He is concerned because their vocal presence was causing problems for everyone – undermining people's faith and taking them away from Christ. Jude says it does matter what you believe, for what you believe affects how you live, and how you live affects you for eternity. Do not think that God is always forgiving and unconditionally loving and merciful. There are times when even God's patience runs out and his concern for those being corrupted comes to the fore.

## Three examples as warnings (verses 5–7)

▶ **The former slaves**, those in the wilderness, whom God had released from slavery in Egypt, rebelled and disobeyed God. They worshipped other gods and disregarded the Ten Commandments – they thought they knew better and they said it didn't matter. But it did matter and God would not let any of them enter the Promised Land. They wandered in the wilderness for forty years until there was a new generation who would follow God's leading.

▶ **Even angels** who disobeyed God, possibly referring to Genesis 6:1–3 where the angels lusted after the beautiful women that they saw, did not keep their place before God. They disobeyed God, incurring his anger, and were punished for failing to do what was right. If even angels are punished when they rebel, what hope is there for people?

▶ **The beautiful towns of the plains**, Sodom and Gomorrah, were well watered and prosperous, but instead of praising and thanking their Creator for all that he had given them, they became arrogant and uncaring, pleasing themselves, ignoring the poor and needy, and guilty in the end of attempted gang rape of any visitors to their town (Genesis 19).

Jude warns his readers that if God deals with former slaves, angels and cities in such a way, we should be careful: careful that we don't become the objects of God's judgment and anger. It is not a comfortable situation to be in.

## Defend the faith from whom?

There are so many ideas that infiltrate our churches: woolly, well-meaning but false ideas. Ideas such as: 'if you are good you are OK with God'; 'all religions lead to God; they are just different paths to get there'; 'our beliefs and ideas about right and wrong are relative to our culture'.

Christian faith needs defending from those who reject absolute truth, who suggest biblical truth is myth, who compromise and bend the teaching of Jesus to fit their own lifestyle.

### How do we defend our faith?

It is very confusing because false teaching does not come with a big red danger sign on it. It comes when we are tired and in need of some excitement. It comes like advertising, telling us everything we want to hear and leaving out everything we don't want to hear. It tells us that we can do what we want and live how we want.

We defend the faith by knowing the truth and holding on to it, by recognizing that God's grace, his kindness and forgiveness, his love and compassion are not to be abused. The false teachers knew of God's grace but they turned it into a licence to do the worst things

Sometimes we have to contend or fight for the faith in our minds. Thoughts come at us from all directions and we must hold on to Christ as Saviour and Lord. We must bring our uncertainties and confusion to him in prayer, and wrestle with them until we are certain of what is right. It is a never-ending fight. We live in a context where our faith is under threat from one corner or another, and it is often difficult to hold on to it, but that is what we must do.

### Questions

1. 'Contend for the faith' (verse 3) makes faith sound like a defined set of beliefs. What would you say are the non-negotiable features of Christian faith that you would fight for, even until death if necessary?
2. Ungodly people have infiltrated the church community to whom Jude writes. Do you think such people could infiltrate the church today? Have you had any experience of such activity?
3. There are three examples of sinful behaviour referred to

in verses 5–7. What point is Jude seeking to make that is relevant to every generation of worshippers?

**Stop and Look:**
**Jude – what we know and what we don't**

Who was Jude and to whom was he writing? The first part is a little easier than the second.

Jude was the half-brother of Jesus and the brother of James, Simeon and Joseph. This may surprise you; some people have never thought about whether Jesus had brothers and sisters. Jude was Jesus' younger half-brother, Mary and Joseph being his parents. He is mentioned in the Gospels, for example in Matthew 13:55.

There is something rather modest about Jude. He could claim the same biological mother as the Messiah, but he does not give that any weight. For Jude, it was inadequate to have known Jesus physically or even to have grown up with him. He knew that the most important thing is to acknowledge Jesus' lordship and his divinity. No-one is exempt from discipleship, and Jude, even as the Messiah's half-brother, still sees himself first and foremost as a servant of the King of Kings. He makes no claim to be an apostle; his highest claim is that the readers are his dear friends. One of the intriguing facts recorded about him suggests that his grandsons were dismissed by the Emperor Domitian when he was informed that they were of Jewish descent.

It is difficult to be precise about who the letter was written to. It could have been any one of a number of small Christian communities in Syria, Asia Minor or Egypt. However, it is reasonably certain that the readers were Jewish Christians, struggling in a Gentile environment and wrestling with subversive teaching within the church. There are many allusions in the letter to Jewish literature and history, which only make sense if the readers have that background.

The main issue within the church was that Christian freedom was being misrepresented as freedom from rules and laws of any kind, which led to immoral behaviour and an unwillingness to acknowledge the lordship of Christ. The corrupt teachers misrepresented Christ, portraying him as a saviour who was indifferent to sensual sins of greed and sexual immorality and always willing to forgive.

# Jude 8–16

## Warning: false teaching could damage your health

**False teachers show their ignorance by being like the worst examples from the Old Testament and failing to note the good example of Michael.**

 Why are there so many empty church buildings in the West? Places where people once worshipped and knew a vibrant community based on the dynamic life of the gospel. Could it be that well-intentioned but false ideas have entered the community and rotted it from the inside? Could it be that not-so-well-intentioned false teachers have infiltrated the believers, and the truth of the gospel has been compromised? There are many reasons why churches die and for some it is a social issue, not necessarily a spiritual issue, but for others it is the shameless teaching and behaviour of leaders and teachers who lead the congregation down a blind alley of unbiblical belief causing the church to die. Jude wants to prevent that from happening to the church to whom he writes.

Jude wrote his letter at a time of social uncertainty and political instability. Jerusalem had fallen to the Romans about ten years earlier, and the church which had been centred on Jerusalem had been scattered with no central leadership or authority. Many of the communities of Christians around the Roman Empire were vulnerable to false ideas and teaching. If you can imagine your denomination's leadership being forced to flee with no easy communications or support systems in place, you can see how isolated Christian communities could be vulnerable and an easy target for all kinds of teachings.

Jude condemns those who had infiltrated the church and shows how they reveal their error. They were sexually immoral, rejecting the authority of the church and claiming to have superior understanding, knowledge and insight; they had no humility and slandered spiritual powers and angelic beings. Jude compares the false teachers to a much greater being than themselves, the archangel Michael, who did not even dare to rebuke the devil himself. Michael had a healthy respect for evil and wrongdoing and left the judgment to God, unlike the infiltrators who had little understanding of anything spiritual.

At the time Jude was writing there was a well-known document, the *Assumption of Moses*, which included this account of when the devil accused Moses of murder and said therefore he could not go into heaven. Michael knew that this accusation was slanderous but he did not presume to condemn the devil and referred the matter to God himself. Unlike the archangel Michael, the false teachers showed no respect for any authority – angels or God. They understood very little of the powers of the heavenly realms – all they seemed to understand was the power of their sex drive and their greed for money.

Writing to this mainly Jewish community, Jude continues in his letter with illustrations from the Old Testament to reinforce his point. The false teachers are like Cain who murdered his brother, or like Balaam who because of greed led God's people into terrible failure before God. Or they are like Korah who contested Moses' authority, questioned God's law and led God's people against him. The false teachers are like the worst examples from Israelite history, and they would be punished by God.

### Further condemnation (verses 12–13)

Jude takes the accusation further and you can begin to understand why Jude is not always a popular letter; he focuses mainly on the threats there are to the faith of the church community. He accuses the infiltrators of being 'blemishes at your love feasts' – the fellowship meal at the heart of the community. The believers would have shared a meal including bread and wine. The false teachers participated despite having been involved in the most abominable activities. Jude likens them to shepherds who, instead of caring about their sheep, encourage them to go astray and get lost. They care nothing for the sheep but look after only their own interests. They are like clouds without rain, appearing to offer life-giving refreshment, but they offer nothing, just leave people with an incredible thirst. They are autumn trees with no fruit, uprooted and dead – a double failure. They bore no fruit and they themselves were dead and wasted. He goes on to describe them as uncontrolled waves of the sea or wandering stars going nowhere. Jude has no sympathy for the false teachers because the threat is so great. They threaten the life of the community of the church and the salvation of the people; this is not a small matter.

### Enoch's warning (verses 14–16)

Enoch would have been known to the community to whom Jude writes. There was an apocryphal book named after him, which warned that God would denounce and punish those who led others astray. Those who have perverted the gospel and spoken against God would be dealt with by God. All that they have said of others will be turned against them. These people think they are the only ones who are right; they boast about themselves and flatter those they want to influence. They grumble about the apostles and authentic leadership in order to boost their own importance. These so-called leaders belong with the condemned of all ages and are not to be admired as some spiritual elite.

## Phoney teachers today

There are attractive ideas and teaching today that can persuade and seduce us, unless we are wise and alert and hold tight to what is right. It might be those who teach an informal attitude to sexuality, arguing that biblical teaching is narrow-minded and repressive. Or it could be those who suggest that all religions lead to God by different routes and that absolute Christian claims are arrogant and bigoted. Or it might be teaching that God wants us to be healthy, wealthy and happy, and that Christian teaching about suffering and hardship is defeatist.

Like the false teachers condemned by Jude, false teachers today offer a false gospel which sounds convincing but is empty and destructive. The only way to find true peace with God and transforming power is the genuine gospel message. Only God's truth offers the love and hope, security and peace that we all hunger and thirst after.

## Questions

1. What was it about the archangel Michael that was impressive? How can we learn from his example?
2. Are there movements or teaching today that are like 'shepherds who feed only themselves ... clouds without rain ... trees without fruit and uprooted – twice dead ... wild waves of the sea'? Think, as you consider this question, about the philosophy and values that are the basis for education, business, science and technology.

3. Who are the scoffers in our generation of whom Enoch and the apostles warn?

# Jude 17–23

## How can we thrive?

---

**Principles for being a thriving disciple of Jesus Christ and principles for mission**

---

Jude began his letter with an encouragement, reminding his readers they are loved, kept and called as those who belong to Jesus Christ. However, he then focused on the less comfortable theme of condemning false teachers for their empty and destructive ways. Now he turns to more positive matters as he concludes his letter.

Even though the false teachers are a serious threat, the believers can take simple steps to keep themselves faithful to God. They shouldn't be surprised about those who disregard godly behaviour and holiness; the apostles and Jesus himself warned that there would be those who would mock belief and faith and try to belittle those who hold to biblical truth. These false teachers would be led by their feelings, appetites and ambitions, pretending some higher spiritual basis to their lifestyle, when in fact it is just their human instinct and impulses taking them in godless ways.

Jude encourages his readers with ways forward to protect their faith and to keep themselves walking with God. His advice crosses the centuries and is useful to those facing the same difficulties as those believers in the first century.

## Four instructions (verses 20–21)

▶ **Build yourself up in your most holy faith** – build into daily routines the opportunities to learn more, understand further and hold on more tightly to the truth of the gospel. Learn to live by the principles and ideas that come from God and have the power to transform, save and protect. There are times when faith is fragile and vulnerable like a priceless piece of glass, but the gospel is robust and tough, and the strength of its truth can empower and keep secure. The thinking, motives, actions, consciences and imagination of those who follow Christ should all be shaped and moulded by biblical ideals. This is a life-long activity; they were to keep on being built up; they were to keep on holding on. The first sign of not being built up in faith is when Christians try to stand alone, thinking they do not need fellowship; they are cut off from spiritual nurture and encouragement. For a leader the danger is when he or she says they don't need to hear from others, they can hear directly from the Holy Spirit. They become isolated and un-accountable.

▶ **Pray in the Spirit** – all Christians have the Holy Spirit and can pray in the Spirit. Praying in the Spirit means allowing God's agenda to be the determining factor in prayer and not personal interests or selfish ambitions. Prayers of praise and worship, of seeking God's will and his purposes are all part of praying in the Spirit. Jesus taught that all things should be brought to God in prayer, and as we become more experienced in prayer, the Holy Spirit brings aware-ness of the difference between the way things should be and the way they are, and takes us deeper in prayer. Jude encourages us to persevere with prayer and to sense increasingly that we are praying what God wants, rather than things that come from our personal self-interest. When we are routinely praying in the Spirit, we will be alert to false ideas that might compromise our faith; we will know 'what God's will is; his good, pleasing and perfect will' (Romans 12:2).

▶ **Keep in God's love** – Jesus himself said, 'If you love me, you will obey what I command' (John 14:15). Keeping in God's love begins with obedience; it means having a relationship that respects and honours God and his ways. Any relationship needs respect and honour: husband and wife, parent and child, friends – love finds a way of showing honour and respect and in return receives friendship, comfort and support. How much more, then, with our relationship with God? We should obey not out of a gritted teeth determination to do what God says, but out of a loving response to God who loves us and only wants what is best for us.

▶ **Wait in hope** for God's purposes to be fulfilled. Jude recognizes that times are tough for his little church community, but they must be patient and wait with hope for God's merciful purposes to come about. Micah, the Old Testament prophet, saw the Israelites abandoning God wholesale. Today we see people deserting God's ways en masse. In the words of Micah, we should say 'But as for me, I watch in hope for the LORD, I wait for God my Saviour; my God will hear me' (Micah 7:7). It is discouraging when it seems as if we are a minority voice, and it is tempting to give in and join the crowd, but Jude encourages us to wait, knowing that our hope is not futile.

Having given four instructions for staying faithful, Jude now gives three suggestions for mission (verses 22–23).

▶ **Be compassionate** to those who question, challenge and struggle, those on the fringes of faith and belief. Don't pigeonhole people as heretics or failures, but be understanding and welcoming.

▶ **Grab from danger** those playing with fire, who are close to abandoning the truth; recognize their vulnerability and find ways in prayer and action to snatch them from what might destroy them. If necessary, use fear of judgment and God's anger to bring them to their senses and remind them of what they have known but have conveniently forgotten.

▶ **Love them, hate their actions,** particularly those who seem to be in danger of changing God's grace into a licence for immorality. Help and encourage them as much as you are able, but don't be tempted by their example.

Jude's advice in these verses is a reminder that being a Christian requires effort and perseverance, and reaching out to others needs generosity and strength.

## Questions

1. What does it mean to build yourself up in your faith? Reflect and remind yourself of what is involved and what is helpful.
2. Is it possible for a church community to find that when it prays it is not 'praying in the Spirit'?
3. How can Jude's words in verses 22–23 aid global mission?

## Stop and look: Perseverance

We live in a time when everything seems to be disposable, whether it is cups and plates, marriages and parenting responsibilities, or faith and beliefs. The encouragement to be flexible and to cope readily with change makes it too easy to give up at times when things are difficult or challenging with the excuse that they don't fit with our lifestyle or priorities.

For the church to whom Jude wrote life was not easy.

They lived in uncertain times and they did not receive the regular teaching and fellowship that might have helped them during their difficulties. Jude encouraged them to persevere with what they had proved in the past to be true and right. So many new ideas were around that it was easy to take a short cut path and find less demanding ways of living for Christ.

Jude urged them to persevere; to keep on with what they know of Christian truth. All of us, at times, go through tough patches, and the temptation is always to give up or give in. The words of Jude encourage us to keep on trying, to have faith, to persist and to continue in those things that we know please God. Some people have to persevere for years or even a lifetime, and that is hard, and yet the mystery of God's purposes will be revealed and the perseverance will be shown to be worth it.

Difficulties come our way for many reasons, but if we face them with perseverance, they can both demonstrate and build our character. How do we learn patience except by persevering with situations that make us impatient? How do we prove the truth of God's grace in every situation except by trusting God whatever is happening?

To persevere these days is to go against the tide of culture. It is not to be guided by your feelings, appetites or desire for comfort and ease. It is to hold on to God even when it doesn't feel so good or isn't so easy, but knowing it is the right thing to do.

**Heresy**

Any teaching which denies an aspect of established doctrine might be called heresy, and throughout the history of the church there have been those who have taught views which don't accord with accepted biblical teaching, although it has to be recognized that Christianity in its earliest days was regarded as a heresy within Judaism.

In the letter of Jude the particular heresies that are condemned are to do with the person of Jesus Christ. The heretical teachers were refusing to accept the lordship of Christ, and were turning teaching on God's forgiveness and mercy into a licence to do whatever they wanted.

The problem with heresy is that it is often attractively packaged and persuasively presented, and it appeals to us for a variety of reasons. It might appeal to our sensual nature and our readily tempted feelings, or it might appeal because it seems to be a softer approach to difficult ethical or pastoral issues. While on the surface heresy may offer an easy way forward, in the long term it is damaging and destructive and undermines the true work of the gospel.

Peter's letters identify false teachers who seemed to have had true faith in the authentic gospel to begin with, but have meandered away from what is right. Compromised behaviour often leads to compromised teaching. The false teachers have given in to sensuality (2 Peter 2:19–20), and then they deny the lordship of Christ. Having behaved inappropriately there is a deliberate rejection of truth

Today there are many ideas and teachings that parade as Christian truth but are, in fact, heresies. There are those who teach that God wants his followers to have material wealth and prosperity, or that doing wrong doesn't matter because we can be forgiven. With most heresies, the teaching begins with an appearance of truth or a half-truth that seems to have some basis in biblical teaching, but the damaging effect of the ideas becomes apparent, when a little thought is given.

**Stop and look:**
**The Apocrypha, Pseudepigrapha and Jude**

In writing this letter, Jude illustrates what he is saying with incidents and events that would have been familiar

to his readers, just as a preacher or writer might do today. Jude alludes to the *Assumption of Moses* (verse 9) and he also quotes from the *Book of Enoch* (verses 14–15). These writings are often referred to as being 'apocryphal'. In other words, while they are respected and valuable for gaining understanding, they don't have the authority of being inspired by God as do the Scriptures.

The Apocrypha is the term given to twelve books written during the Old Testament era and the time between the testaments, which are approved as worthy of study and understanding but are not as commendable for reading and use in worship as the books of the Bible (the canon of Scripture). The *Assumption of Moses* and the *Book of Enoch* appear in the texts known as the Pseudepigrapha and not in the twelve books that form the Apocrypha.

There are fragments of the manuscript of the *Book of Enoch* in Latin, Aramaic and Hebrew. It was thought to have been written during the first or second century BC. The *Assumption of Moses* is referred to by other authors at various points, which is how its existence is known, but only a fragment of an eleventh-century manuscript actually exists today.

The Apocrypha contains writings of varying styles and focus. There is literature similar to the Old Testament wisdom writings, including the 'Debate of the Three Youths' in *1 Esdras*, a fascinating discussion about which is the most powerful – wine, women or truth. Another apocryphal work such as *Judith* is intriguing, as it shows the courage of a widow who uses cunning to defeat an enemy, but the work is probably fictitious.

Those books which make up the Pseudepigrapha were not considered worth including in either the Old Testament canon or in the Apocrypha. Pseudepigrapha means 'published under another's name', which is not strictly true of all the documents included in this classification, but it shows that such writings were excluded because they were deemed to be falsely ascribed to more trustworthy writers or not as credible as other writings. Since most of the pseudepigraphal works are dated between the Testaments, they offer huge insight into the thinking of various groups at that time. The *Book of Jubilees* suggests a legalistic approach to the calendar in order to assist in the celebration of religious feasts and is an attempt to stem the tide of Greek influence. *3 Maccabees* is a record of Jewish life under Ptolemy Physcon in Egypt, and seeks to give a glowing account of Jewish life and action during that time. *4 Maccabees* was written by a Jew who had been influenced by Greek philosophy, and was an attempt to show how passions could be restrained and controlled by reason.

Just as writers and preachers today use a wide variety of resources to gain understanding and to communicate effectively, so the writers and speakers of the first century had access to various source materials of varying quality that could aid them in their thinking and communication. The Apocrypha and Pseudepigrapha continue to be useful sources of wisdom and understanding and are worthy of respect, although not at the level of Scripture.


# Jude 24–25

A golden goodbye!

---

**The final verses of Jude's letter contain one of the most graphic depictions of God in his wonder and brilliance, reassuring his readers that they can be bold and confident in their faith.**

---

In his final words, Jude, conscious he has said some fairly harsh things, comes back to the place where he started – the amazing and overwhelming presence of the Sovereign Lord of the universe. The letter has a power-packed opening and a staggering ending, with lots of instructions in the middle about where things are going wrong. It is a sandwich the wrong way round, where the outside bits are the most interesting and exciting, and the middle bit is necessary, but not so enjoyable.

Having written about the troubles and difficulties faced by the church, Jude reminds his readers of God who can be trusted; God in whom they can have confidence; God who is with them and will always be with them.

**He is able (verse 24):** this is not some minor deity able to sort out only a few problems, but he is the King of the universe, the Sovereign Lord who is able to protect and keep his people and to present them pure and holy for eternity. He is competent; he has the proficiency to do all that is needed and far more.

**He is the only God (verse 25):** he the only one who can give hope and a place in eternity. There are many who claim to be able to help, but only God truly is able. People seek help and solutions in many ways, but find after searching and struggling that the one God is the only one who gives peace.

**He is the Saviour (verse 25):** it is interesting how many people think they don't need saving from anything. Most people are quick to deny any need of help and prefer to be independent. To admit they need support or saving would be a little offensive; it is to suggest that they are weak or flawed.

The truth is that everyone does need saving. For some it is obvious – an addiction, bad behaviour patterns, self-pity or bitterness; for others it may be circumstances or situations that are out of control, but we all need saving so we can know the forgiveness and love that only God can give. It is so easy to perceive ourselves as 'fine', but the corruptive impact of sin makes salvation an urgent necessity for us all.

### The superlative God (verse 25)

In this final verse there are four words that try to do the impossible – to paint a picture of God: God who defies description because he is so great; God who cannot be understood because he is so much greater than finite understanding.

**He is glorious:** God has glory. He created a wonderful, beautiful world that gives an inkling of his brilliance. His radiance is seen in sunsets and dawns, in grand mountains and awesome waterfalls, in glaciers and oceans, in rich green valleys and in rainbows, in the sound of the sparrow and the grandeur of the elephant. If he can create all of that, what does this say about God himself? The Creator is glorious not only in his creativity but in his love and compassion, his mercy and grace. This is the God of Christian faith. So awesome and marvellous that even thinking about him is difficult.

**Majesty:** he is magnificent, splendid and dignified; he is royalty above all royals. Adjectives such as regal, imperial, stately and noble are all correctly ascribed to God, along with holy and just, righteous and pure. This is our God, worthy of worship and praise, able to walk with his people, and yet worthy of all honour, tribute, respect and admiration.

**He is powerful:** detergents claim to be powerful. They claim to have strength and astonishing ability to clean grime, and some of them do manage to do the job effectively. But what about cleaning up the world? What about cleaning up the hatred and evil, the greed and the arrogance? God is powerful in working from the inside out. He is able to take the worst of people and transform them, as well as bring down governments and those who think themselves so great. God's power makes the most damaging bomb look like a children's toy. The strength of the ocean and winds, the currents and the storm are nothing compared to the force and might of God the Creator.

**Authority:** God has the right to command for he is the Lord of everything. He is the one who holds power and so he has authority. He can do as he pleases and he pleases to be loving and gracious, kind and compassionate to all who respond to him. He is his own authority, for he is the Lord and he needs neither the affirmation nor the acceptance of others. He is the ultimate authority. It is to him that everyone and everything is answerable. His is the authority that has the final word.

God is glorious, majestic, powerful and authoritative. This is the Lord of the universe, who is able to make and keep promises and he promises two things: 'to keep you from falling and to present you before his glorious presence without fault and with great joy' (verse 24).

### To keep you from falling

Those who trust in God through Christ will be kept in love and peace. Those who hold on to God's presence will be protected from the spiritual disasters that would be faced by the false teachers mentioned earlier.

Jude has told his readers to build themselves up, to pray, to stay in God's love and to wait in hope, but now he focuses on the support and strength they will receive from God. None of their efforts will be fruitless and none of their sacrifices will be empty gestures; they will be fit for God, kept for eternity, held for heaven, not because of themselves, but because of God's love for them shown in Christ.

God is able to protect from harm, from the inner pain of isolation, discord, bitterness and resentment. At times their journey of faith would have seemed like a marathon, over rough terrain with danger and threats all round. At times the believers may have felt there was no guarantee they would stay on course and reach the finish. Would they fail, would it all end in disaster? Jude says of course not.

It is not about them clinging on to faith, for God is holding on to them and will never let go. He is holding on to them in the depths of their inner being, so that even in the most testing of circumstances they are kept pure and safe.

Jude encourages his readers to have a vision of God that gives the comfort and strength to continue, even in the most desperate of circumstances. Many believers worry that they won't end the race of faith well, that something will happen to trip them up and they will fail. The doubts and the difficulties that threaten to overwhelm are not uncommon, but this promise reminds all Christians that God will keep safely for eternity all those who respond to him.

## To present you

The prophet Malachi (3:2) sums up what many of us may feel. When we understand how great God is, his majesty and glory, his awesome wonder and power, who can stand before him? Who can endure the day of his coming? We who are so aware of our failings and our shortcomings, how can we stand before the holy and powerful God?

In high society when a girl reached a certain age, she had her coming out; she was presented to society and, depending on her sponsor, she would come out expensively or modestly. All Christians will be presented to God, and the one who sponsors them and introduces them to eternity is Jesus Christ himself. There is no fear of not being accepted.

God keeps his people so that he might present them perfect, sinless and innocent before himself. The people to whom Jude wrote were conscious of being amongst those who threatened to contaminate them, and we too might feel that we live in a world that encourages our worst side and leads us down paths of which we are not proud. God sees everything, but he can present those who trust in him as perfect and forgiven.

God is able to keep you, to present you, because he is more awesome than you could ever imagine, more powerful and willing than you would think possible. This is the God Jude trusts and in whom we can have confidence.

**Questions**

1. Reflect for a moment on the words Jude uses to paint an amazing picture of God. What detail of this picture most inspires you?
2. Has the church focused sufficiently on God's willingness to keep and present his people without fault, or is there a danger that the church has concentrated more on the failures of people before God?
3. The world seems to be an increasingly joyless place, as people are afraid of using humour or laughter in case it is regarded as politically incorrect or viewed with suspicion. What does the emphasis on joy in the Bible tells us about Christian life and values?

# Further reading

I. Howard Marshall, *1 Peter* (IVP, 1991) – a comprehensive and easy-to-read detailed commentary on the background and truth of Peter's first letter. A good resource for preachers and those wanting to dig even more deeply.

S. McKnight, *The NIV Application Commentary: 1 Peter* (Zondervan, 1996) – a detailed application of the teaching of Peter in his first letter. Valuable insights for those particularly concerned to make the Bible relate to life situations today.

E. Clowney, *The Message of 1 Peter* (IVP Bible Speaks Today Series, 1988) – a thorough and valuable resource for those seeking to grasp in depth and detail the message of 1 Peter.

R. Lucas and C. Green, *The Message of 2 Peter and Jude* (IVP Bible Speaks Today Series, 1995) – a good resource for those wishing to understand some of the complexities of these two letters in greater depth. Clearly written with the preacher/teacher in mind.